Evyn, M... this book
provide...
on your way ... ...
God in all things

Jessica Hootn Wlsn
11/12/19

AMBITION

AMBITION

Essays by members of
The Chrysostom Society

WITH AN INTRODUCTION BY

Scott Cairns

EDITED BY

Luci Shaw & Jeanne Murray Walker

CASCADE *Books* • Eugene, Oregon

AMBITION

Cascade Books
An Imprint of Wipf and Stock Publishers
199 W. 8th Ave., Suite 3
Eugene, OR 97401

www.wipfandstock.com

ISBN 13: 978-1-62564-134-2

Cataloging-in-Publication data:

    Ambition / The Chrysostom Society ; edited by Luci Shaw and Jeanne Murray Walker.

    xii + 142 p.; 23 cm.

    ISBN 13: 978-1-62564-134-2

    1. Ambition 2. Humility 3. Spirituality—Christian. I. Shaw, Luci. II. Walker, Jeanne Murray. III. Title.

HF5386 .A16 2015

Manufactured in the USA.

to those whose ultimate goal has been reached—
Doris Betts, Madeleine L'Engle, Keith Miller, and Robert Siegel

Contents

CONTENTS

Introduction

AMBITION? WELL, I'M ALL for it. Strongly in favor.

That is to say that I am strongly in favor of *genuine* ambition, which as far as I can tell comes down to a powerful and continuing desire to accomplish genuinely great things—or even, perhaps, to *become* a great thing, a genuinely great artist, a great poet, or a great *whatever*.

Bringing their greatly various experiences, estimable insight, and uncommon honesty to the matter, the contributors to the present volume have offered a detailed appraisal of this particular species of human desire, and they offer us a particularly useful understanding as to why so many of us may have felt ambivalent about ambition, *per se*. It is, after all, an impulse that can lead either to greatness or to ruin.

In a savory, writerly stroll regarding her own, personal experiences, an insightful discussion of technique versus vision, and a very profound "theology of daily living," **Erin McGraw's** perspicuity and even-handedness—"ambition as it relates to vice, and as it permits excellence"—posits, from the start, that ambition, *per se*, is a mostly neutral quality; the extent to which it is good or bad pretty much depends upon the goal—the *what* for which one is ambitious.

Bringing both her famous compassion and unwavering candor to bear upon the matter, **Luci Shaw** recounts her own ambivalence regarding literary accomplishment and acknowledgment, and offers a series of helpful observations from an array of authors as she settles on something of a test to determining the efficacy of one's ambition: *does it serve*?

Emilie Griffin also presents—also with compassion, wit, and keen intelligence—an account of her own wrestling with the lure of "Fame," as she recounts the incremental manner in which most of us eventually come to terms with ambition and responsibility.

Calling upon the insights of Shakespeare, Alexis de Tocqueville, Machiavelli, and others, **Dain Trafton** moves to how his own confusions have stemmed from—on the one hand—his family's pronounced respect for ambition and—on the other hand—his early exposure to what were ostensibly biblical condemnations of the same; he concludes with a narrative that contains a thoughtful commentary on the latter.

Eugene Peterson writes of the tensions between busyness and ambition, and draws upon the wisdom of certain literary authors who have helped him to recover and to retain a healthy ambition—paired with a mitigating humility—regarding the work before us.

Wrestling with the particular ambivalences that accompany the gender-specific challenges of a woman with ambitions, **Jeanne Murray Walker** attends to the further complication of one's having ambitions—acknowledged or not—for one's children.

With confident recourse to scriptural models and desk references alike, **Diane Glancy** provides something of an *apologia* for ambition. She is grateful for it, sees it as a gift. "I would have been wiped out," she writes, "if it weren't for ambition." Even so, she appears to have blended that ambition with humility, a confidence in the One who has given her such gifts.

Gina Ochsner offers an entertaining appraisal of ambition's insatiability, how one ambition—duly accomplished—nearly always leads to escalation of what one desires.

Finally, in a brilliant bit of bait and switch, **Bret Lott** presents a chastening reminder of how much more satisfying our ambitions—those we realize *and* those for which we still struggle—become when they take a back seat to gratitude, a deep sense of having been blessed.

꩜

As for me, I have come to think that the matter of our moment comes down to our responding with adequate energy to a *God-given* desire to become what each one of us is called to become, which is *holy*. That is, of course, an immensely grand ambition.

I'll get back to that vertiginous aspect of our persons in a moment; for now, let's account for some of our habits of thinking that ambition is something to be avoided, or something for which one must apologize.

Like most writers who have been involved for any significant length of time in "the writing life," I've met a writer or two (maybe several thousand) in whom ambition appeared to be very acute, but whose ambition was—in my opinion—concurrently meager.

Some of those folks—it seemed to me—manifested what I took to be a colossal ambition for what turned out to be very small things. Some students or conference attendees, for instance, have wanted merely—even if they also wanted desperately—to *publish* something, thereafter, they wanted to publish *more*. Thereafter, they wanted to publish in better and better journals, or with better and better presses.

A number of them have wanted simply to be well known, and thereafter they wanted—so far as such things can even occur in the obscure world of serious literature—to be *famous*; when some had attained what most folks would have recognized as a respectable level of fame, many of them began to worry overmuch about the relative fame of others.

This indicates what I mean when I speak of ambition for small things, a vestige of "Grub Street," a sign of untoward neediness. That is to say, such is *not* the species of ambition that I am holding up as laudable. On the contrary, I hold up this sort of self-aggrandizing disposition as a profound embarrassment. Not grand. Paltry.

So, back to what I would call the *right* sort of ambition.

More than a few of my poetry students have protested when I have said to them—as, frankly, I am fairly quick to say to *all* of them—that if they aren't committed to writing *great* poems they really should get out of the way of those who are.

Some of those students, in fact, *have* been gracious enough to step out of the way. The others, thank God, have responded by appropriately raising the bar for themselves, having understood that this is *precisely* the required measure of our due efforts at poetry, or at fiction, or at any of our art forms: accomplishment, greatness.

Either we are called to greatness, or we are not called at all.

As it happens, I never tell my students that they must write great poems that week, or the next week, the next year, or anytime soon; I simply make it very clear that they must desire, *immediately*, to do so. I simply make it very clear that they must give their every effort at writing a poem precisely *that* kind of serious attention and precisely *that* kind of strenuous effort.

✧

Again: ambition is only bad if it is an ambition for small things.

Ambition for *great* things is itself a *great thing*, an honorable thing, and worthy of those who are shaped in the image of God, those called to acquire His likeness. I would have to say that this sort of ambition is, itself, something of a gift.

And *that*, when all is put on the table, is precisely the point. That God Himself appears to be the One who has placed this desire into our hearts. He is the One who first shaped us in the likeness of Himself, and the One who has called us to grow into His very Image.

Relegated to the periphery over generations of Western theological parsings, *theosis* remains the very heart of our matter and is the essence of the very good news that is the gospel of Christ.

Saint Irenaus states that God "became what we are that we might make us as Himself." Saint Clement observes that through obedience one "becomes a god while still walking in the flesh." Saint Athanasios says, "He assumed our human flesh so that we might assume His divinity." Saint Cyril avers that as we are called "temples of God, and even gods, and so we are." And Saint Gregory Naziansus admonishes us: "Become gods for His sake, since he became man for our sake."

The consensus of the fathers and the mothers of our holy Church has long embraced the good news that the purpose of His coming was not merely to save us from death, but to endow us with life, divine life, His life, endlessly becoming.

This is what I would call an exceedingly healthy ambition. Good journey!

Scott Cairns
University of Missouri

1

What's a Heaven For?

Erin McGraw

A man's worth is no greater than the worth of his ambitions.
MARCUS AURELIUS

I'M SETTING OUT TO write about ambition, and my mind is swimming with the possibilities. Ambition as it relates to vice, and as it permits excellence. Ambition, that pivotal state: it is excellent until it causes its own downfall. King Lear. Richard Nixon. This is going to be my best essay *ever*.

My mother is eighty-eight and losing her mind by agonizing inches. She creates tests for herself to gauge her diminishment; the latest one involves going through her address book, trying to remember each of the names there. Her address book is probably forty years old, and it's lumpy with paper clips and bits of cardboard with notes scrawled on them. Cross outs and arrows show when friends or family members moved, then moved again. A lot of people are listed only by their first names—I think these are hairdressers and manicurists. There are dozens of names that I couldn't identify at gunpoint. Mom squeezes her eyes to think better.

"Damn it," she says, big-time swearing for her. "I should *know* this." The fact that this proud woman is letting me see her struggle tells me how afraid she is.

Her ambition is not just to recognize every name in her address book. Her ambition is to get her lost memory back again, as if it were a runaway dog that she can find if she calls it long and loudly enough. Her ambition is heartbreaking, and it explains why I am brusque with her. "You're doing fine," I say. "Let's get lunch." The next time I visit her, I am going to hide her address book.

Ambition carries us into terrible places. I don't understand why it has such a good reputation. People remark that so-and-so is very ambitious, and we're given to understand that so-and-so is full of drive and moxie. Even when the ambition edges into shadier territory, and we start modifying it with adjectives like "blind" or "ruthless," admiration still clings to our sense of the word. "My. That's an ambitious project," the teacher says to the student who has just announced that she wants to decode the human genome or write a five-volume novel based on a ninth-century Icelandic saga. Bless her heart, she's in way over her head. But you've got to admire her ambition.

Where will she be in six months? Most likely, sunk in a nest of notes and books and web sites. Maybe she'll be grimly trying to chew her way through the task she's set for herself, acknowledging with small despair that she's already months behind the timetable she had set for herself. Maybe she'll already have given up and be playing video games. No matter what, she'll be witnessing the gulf between her ambition and her skills and strength. Like standing at the edge of a chasm that must be crossed, and realizing the length of rope in your hand is only fifteen inches long.

Ambition is a false friend. It encourages us to imagine ourselves bearing home the victory. We hear the cheers from the crowd and see our picture on TV, where we look a good deal better than we usually do in pictures. In the case of particularly triumphant ambition, our enemies and detractors have been pushed to the front of the crowd. There they watch our apotheosis with impotent rage. I've always appreciated the psalmist who included in the rhapsody of the 23rd Psalm not only the gracious pleasures of the Lord, but the incredible satisfaction of having a table set before us in the sight of our foes. If you have an imagination like mine, you can linger on that moment for quite a long, sweet time.

The problem is that eventually we have to return to our regularly scheduled programming. The cat box needs cleaning. The tattered spot on the sofa looks just terrible. We're behind on three projects for work, and we're sick of all of them. We know every single corner and turn of our lives, and they're small and unenviable and dull. The truth is that a lot of our enemies are doing significantly better than we are, and the moments we give in to ambitious daydreaming only serve to point up the tawdry minginess of what we've actually accomplished.

I'm not supposed to think like this. Rightly applied, ambition is the goad that will prod me into getting the sofa reupholstered, and going on not only to finish but to excel at my tasks at work, using them as a launch pad to blast off so that my potential greatness is recognized and rewarded—whoops, I'm daydreaming again. And the cat box still needs cleaned.

Just about any monastic or faith tradition would remind me to keep my eyes trained on what I'm supposed to be doing, to live in the present and let the future take care of itself. A wise 12-step slogan advises us to do our work and stop worrying about results. Sufficient unto the day is the evil thereof. All that.

My mother, if she could remember, would counsel me against ambition. Raised in a small, insular mining town in central Wyoming, she grew up among the boasts and dreams of success, and the derisive laughter when those dreams came spectacularly short. By example more than word, she taught me to play my cards close to the chest. If I was going to be fool enough to be ambitious, I shouldn't let anyone know. That way, if I failed, no one would be in a position to laugh. It's good advice if you don't mind taking it for granted that you're going to fail.

This is a pretty un-American approach. We are people who have founded our identity and tradition on the nearly sacred idea of ambition. What could be more ambitious than the thrilled, lovely hope of a child to be president one day? That's what Jimmy Carter told his mother, adding that he meant president of the United States. When he informed her, she reportedly told him to move his feet from the bed. That's a mother who doesn't truck too much with ambition.

But she didn't get in the way of it, either. Maybe her boy was going to be president of the United States, maybe not. No reason he shouldn't have a shot at it so long as he remembered not to put his feet on the bed.

⊖

We characteristically think of ambition's antonym as humility. "I have not gone after things too great / nor marvels beyond me," says the psalmist in Psalm 131, neatly capturing the issue (v. 1b, REVISED GRAIL PSALTER). If we remember our place, and do not pursue things too great, we will sleep as sweetly as the babe at its mother's breast.

But does any system of morality in its right mind want to keep its citizens from reaching for great things? Even the poet Robert Browning, not exactly a firebrand, said that we should be encouraged to reach out. It's easy to understand his reasoning. As long as we keep trying, trying, trying to grasp what is just beyond our reach, we'll move ourselves forward in knowledge and innovation. In 1855, Browning wrote, "A man's reach should exceed his grasp." The Industrial Revolution was changing the face of the world, and people were learning how the use of steam or coal could make possible large-scale industry, mass production, even transformative technological magic like electricity. Work in an industrial textile mill might not be anybody's idea of heaven, but it was still safer and paid better than farm work, or begging.

"A man's reach should exceed his grasp," Browning wrote, and then next: "Or what's a heaven for?" Well now, that changes things. Once we start bringing the afterlife into the discussion, we tacitly allow that only in heaven will our striving be fulfilled. There's plenty of devotional and theological writing to back this position up, but the happy aphorism takes on a disquieting ring when we apply it to our daily, working lives. Browning seems to be assuring us of failure as soon as we try for greatness. Certainly that was the position of the poem's speaker, Andrea del Sarto. Michelangelo considered him to be the painter with the greatest technique of his time— greater than Leonardo, greater than Raphael, greater than Michelangelo himself. Technique was del Sarto's sublime gift, and his stumbling block. In the luminous company of his time, he could be no more than a superb technician, able to adjust color and shading better than anyone but never able to see the possibilities, the shapes behind the shapes, that illuminated the work of his contemporaries. It's a special kind of hell to have skill but no vision—or, worse, not enough vision. To know that, in the words Browning puts into del Sarto's mouth,

> All is silver-grey,
> Placid and perfect with my art: the worse!

I know both what I want and what might gain,
And yet how profitless to know, to sigh
'Had I been two, another and myself,
'Our head would have o'erlooked the world!'
No doubt.

We don't get to be two. We're locked into our own vision, our own comprehension, our own supplies of courage or dread. Del Sarto already knows that he has chosen not to have the great, leaping vision of his contemporaries, and probably couldn't have had it for the choosing. We can hear his resignation and his bitterness in his own words: "No doubt."

"Want" means not only "desire," but also "lack." For want of a nail, the shoe was lost. To want things emphasizes our lack of them. To reach for things—attainments, knowledge, money—only clarifies our awareness of the distance between the tips of our straining fingers and the objects' dancing, derisive distance, just out of reach.

⊖

"I missed you last week," my mother says. Normally we talk every morning on the phone, she in her home in southern California, I in mine two thousand miles away. For the past week I've been teaching at a conference, and so haven't been available at our usual time.

"We talked three times," I tell her.

"What did we talk about?"

"Blake. Your new great grandson." He was born in every way perfect, except missing his left hand, a birth abnormality that somehow was overlooked on the sonogram at twenty weeks. The family is scrambling to reconfigure and take this in stride.

"I don't remember that," she says fretfully. "I'm not improving as fast as I'd like."

She's said this often enough that I shouldn't be surprised, but I'm still jolted, every time. "You're doing fine, Mom," I say, too late and without conviction.

"I've got to work harder."

"You don't. Really. Just relax and take it easy."

"Where is that going to get me?" she says. There's no answer to that one.

⌁

Softer than an ambition is a dream. A dream has sweetness and grandeur, and it doesn't seem so work oriented. We are not accountable for dreams. The majestic vision of Martin Luther King Jr. would never have left the ground if he had proclaimed, "I have an ambition."

But that's the point, isn't it? Ambition has a reckless, hell-bent-for-leather demeanor. Ambition doesn't have to be cocksure, but it often is. It is dashing, as brash as a top gun. It is fueled by the knowledge that its goals seem unattainable; how it will laugh at the unbelieving world when it accomplishes its aims. One of my favorite *Doonesbury* cartoon strips featured Zonker, the perennially stoned slacker, tending plants in a greenhouse. Because it is a cartoon strip and because Zonker was always high, he had conversations with the plants and the plants talked back. One especially scrappy shrub took a shine to Zonker and confided in him as well as the other plants in the greenhouse. It had big plans, it said. "I'm gonna be a tree, fellas!"

Ambition knows that it's taking a risk. It's always riding for a fall, and this is, again, part of its appeal. Every runner crouched at the starting line has the ambition of victory, and we in the bleachers are genuinely thrilled when we see greatness—a human being running faster than anyone had thought possible. One runner's ambition and attainment can change the world. What a lovely idea that is! One person's attainment enlarges possibility for all of us. This is, taken down to basics, the fundamental idea behind monasticism, or any prayer. But in monastic prayer, action is stripped as far as possible from ambition. Monks offer prayer in the conviction that God, not the guy on his knees in the prayer stall, is the only source of attainment. If we are to believe the autobiographies of saints, nothing works so diligently as prayer to strip us of ambition. God's school appears to give its highest grades to the absence of personal ambition or individual achievement. The more we can lose the trickle of our own desires in the torrent of God's will, the better.

From this comprehension springs a lot of pious literature that sounds, to those who don't understand the transaction at work, unbelievable or puzzling or so overly sweet as to be emetic. It isn't hard to pray, "Your will, Lord, not mine." In fact, it's pretty easy to get lost in the selfless, woozy rapture of that prayer, perhaps pausing along the way to congratulate ourselves on how fantastically holy we're being. It's even easy to make the prayer in sincerity; at those times I think we expand not only our own hearts and souls, but the compassion of the world.

But such pure and selfless prayer is, for most of us, a mountaintop experience, and impure, selfish prayer is as likely to follow as down follows up. Yes, we want God's will to be done. Absolutely. But that desire does not negate our desire for certain aspects of God's will to include our will. In absolute sincerity, I want God's will to be done, and I will try to bend my efforts to effect that Divine will. But if God's will includes the loss or suffering of someone I love, I'm going to have some trouble swallowing it, or praying for the furtherance of God's will. And if God's will includes the loss or suffering of me, I'm really going to have trouble signing off.

⌁

This essay isn't going anything like the way I'd planned. It has lost track of its initial clarity, and it's getting dangerously whiny, like its maker. Once again I've set out to write something that would surpass my usual skills and achievement, and once again I'm confronted with the dismal limitations of my own talents. It's like trying to jump over the wall, only to run face-first into the wall. Over and over and over.

⌁

My mother cried on the phone yesterday. This happens once every week or two, though she doesn't remember that. "I feel like a burden to you," she said. "It must be terrible, having to listen to me just keep repeating the same things. They're not even interesting."

"Of course you're not a burden, Mom." This is true, though I know she is determined not to believe me, and I haven't found the language to convince her otherwise. She is teaching me a number of sad lessons, and I try to hang onto every one of them.

"I can do better than this. I'm going to do better than this."

Today, though, she sounds firmly chipper. "Everything is fine. The time passes here very quickly. Really, I'm not unhappy," she says, though I haven't asked. It's pretty clear whom she is convincing. "Well, I'd better let you get back to whatever you're doing."

"I hope you have a good day," I say. We've been on the phone for less than two minutes. "I love you."

Her voice catches. "I love you, too." She hangs up so fast that I barely catch her last sentence. In her new resolve, there is no room for emotion, which reminds her that she is miserable and frightened and lonely. Who can blame her for fixing her mind instead on her renewed ambition? Ambition abolishes the diminishing thoughts. It replaces them with exciting thoughts, or at least stouthearted ones. It fixes her eyes on a future that is full of promise instead of a present that is rich in fear and disappointment.

She has dementia. The disease goes in only one direction. Her future is not full of promise; her future will be more diminished than her present. I'm not about to remind her of these facts, but they are facts, and her intent to change them by wishing them to be otherwise is nothing more than magical thinking. In other words, ambition is a grand deceiver, the Father of Lies. Ambition is the devil.

❧

Humility isn't the only opposite of ambition. Another equal and opposite force, at least as potent, is complacency. As sins go, complacency is one of the delightful ones, inviting us to loaf and take our ease. Everything is fine, complacency says. There's no need for us to bestir ourselves. Everything is A-OK, except maybe we could stand a refill of our iced tea while we lie out here on the lounge chair.

I'm not confident about many assertions regarding God, but I'm inclined to think that our complacency is one of God's special irritants. Here God puts us in the middle of an inexhaustibly rich life, brimming over with potential no matter what direction we face, and complacency persuades us to take advantage of exactly none of it. It is fatly content. It is lazy. It is contemptible because it bespeaks an absence of faith. Complacency presumes that things aren't going to get any better than they are right now, while faith says that we haven't even started to see what God has up the Divine sleeve.

This fat, purring pleasure represents the happy side of complacency. There's a dreadful side, too. That's the aspect of Janus-faced complacency that says nothing will ever improve, and so we shouldn't waste our energy trying to make things better. This sense hums with fear and a lively appreciation that God, who has all power, could easily make things worse at any moment. Instead of lying out on a lounge chair, this kind of fearfulness crouches behind a bush, afraid to catch God's attention because there's no telling what God might do. In this situation we, who are created in God's image, are made craven. "The stake that sticks up gets hammered down," says the Japanese proverb. I think it must be a sadness to God to see us limit ourselves so.

If we are all stakes eyeing each other to make sure we're not standing so tall as to attract the hammer's attention, then we have very little volition. Our actions have to be made in conformity with those of the stakes around us—no loud laughter, no unusual opinions. No striving. No excellence.

No freedom. Seen from one angle, ambition itself strangles freedom, subsuming habits and desires to the achievement of the goal. Most of us know people like this, and all of us have seen the movies featuring the ruthless schemer who will stop at nothing to get what he has set his twisted heart upon. Iago. Gordon Gecko.

But fear produces enslavement, too, the cautious looking around before we try out an opinion or an outfit, the nervous measuring of ourselves against those around us. Prisoners in POW camps learn early and hard not to be the tall stake. So ambition, in one sense, restricts us, but complacency restricts us more and worse. For crying out loud, isn't there a middle path?

I teach college, and so I see a lot of ambition. Students, especially graduate students, are self-selected for ambition, and sometimes confide in their professors, hoping for guidance, wisdom, and a letter of recommendation. In those letters, I often mention ambition, taking care to note that so-and-so demonstrates "the best kind of ambition." This phrase suggests there can be a worst kind of ambition, and there can. The worst kind of ambition inheres in wanting to publish a book not so that you can explore issues of significance or add to the store of wisdom in the world, but so that other people will look up to you, so that you'll get invited to the best parties, and so that you'll get to date celebrities. We all know this, I think. The worst kind of ambition seeks reputation even, as Shakespeare reminds us, in the cannon's mouth.

The best kind of ambition smiles patiently at the idea of parties and isn't much interested in celebrities. It aims to create something worthy and lasting. It aims to be able to sit back in satisfaction, like our Maker, and be able to say about its creation, "It is good." In fact—why be abashed? Why not admit this?—it wants to be able to say, "It is great." I want to make something great. There, I've said it.

The silence that surrounds that sentence is horrifying. "All right then, get cracking. You want to make something great. Get on with it." And what is there to do except smile with embarrassment, like the clown who pulls his pockets inside out only to find nothing in them but air?

Many years ago I wrote a novel about a female minister in southern Indiana who gets involved with the abortion rights struggle. The book's embrace was wide; it depicted conservative and liberal approaches to the ministry, conservative and liberal ideas about abortion, consideration of marriage, theology, ethics, and one remarkably snarky teenage character who was a lot of fun to write. I poured everything I cared about into that novel, particularly my belief in an abiding, forgiving God at the center of every human activity. It was the biggest book I've ever written, pulsing with ambition. Still, even I wasn't so dazzled by my own creation as to think that it would vault to the top of best-seller lists, over celebrity cookbooks and splashy memoirs. What I could imagine was the kind of book that quietly gains traction as more and more attentive, sensitive readers found it and saw there a book of worth. I could imagine such a scenario very clearly. I imagined it over and over, and imagined myself at the National Book Awards ceremony. I imagined the beautifully cut jacket I would wear.

Anyone can see where this story is going. I wrote a book that contained everything I care about, that talked with no small passion about those things, and that put my heart on the line. Then I discovered that very few people cared about my heart or its issues. My interests were my interests, and were shared by precious few others. The book struggled to find a publisher, struggled to find readers, and swiftly went out of print. I was heartbroken.

My error was not only ambition, I think now, but also hubris. If I had not been caught up in dreams of success and instead had focused only on my writing, the portion of the work that was within my control, I wouldn't have set myself up for such hurt. This seems indisputable, and it's true that I learned my lesson. I have never since engaged in fond daydreams of a certain splashy kind of literary success. I approach those daydreams the way I approach an open flame. Turn it down! This is not a moral or religious choice. It's the reaction, to switch the metaphor, of a soldier who has lost an arm in battle when she hears an explosion close by. She wants to flee.

Still, ambition was part of the problem, too. Not only did I want that National Book Awards ceremony, I wanted to reach readers about issues of passionate importance to me. I didn't want to force anybody to change her mind, but I wanted people to listen. That, I think, is a pretty solid ambition, and one at which I failed entirely. For the next book, my agent suggested that I go more mainstream.

And I did. That's what we do; that's what we are taught to do. Jesus fell three times on his way to Calvary. The point of our remembering this, I was taught, was not that Jesus fell but that he got up again. Most of us who've been alive for more than a year know all about falling down and getting up.

Sometimes falling is exhilarating, and exactly what we crave. Skydiving. Trampolines. Bungee jumping. To feel ourselves in free fall is spectacular. For once we aren't trying to keep ourselves upright and proper. Instead, we can give into the beauty of what gravity does, allowing our weight to pull us toward the ground that wants us, knowing that just this once, we won't be hurt. What is the ambition of a skydiver? To fall spectacularly. Maybe that's what really good ambition looks like. It knows all about the fall. It embraces the fall. It wants the fall.

Or maybe I'm getting this all wrong.

❧

Sufis say that if you want something in your life, you should increase your need for it. I think this runs parallel to old advice to write a good poem: Purify the source.

Even if we bridle a little at the idea we need purification, the advice is still good. If we cleanse our vision and put aside clutter, we're more likely to achieve work that we're proud of, springing from our best self, than if we attempt to peer through our dusty old, normal vision. Good soil produces good plants. But cleansing the vision is not as easy as digging compost into the garden.

If we want to step away from toxic ambition, what do we replace it with? I'm not sure that going from "I want to make a million dollars" to "I want to be a warrior for God" is necessarily an improvement if it is even psychologically feasible. Just how, exactly, does a person go about being a warrior for God? Where's the rulebook for that?

I once knew a woman who was finishing a graduate degree in public health education with the intention of working in the Third World to improve health conditions in Southeast Asia. Commendable, right? Generous. Warrior-for-God-ish. When I met her at a camp in the Philippines, I thought I'd never seen a stiffer, more uncomfortable person.

Before the first week of her class was over, her students—adults, most of them older than their teacher—were complaining. "She treats us like we're in kindergarten!" they said. When they asked questions in the classroom, she answered in one-syllable words, pointing to the textbook the students had already read; the question wasn't answered there.

I watched her in the dining room, where she flinched away from easygoing gestures or touch. When people laughed at jokes, she shuddered and drew back. When the whole group went to a festival, she opted to stay in the truck. Once I saw her sitting outside the classroom with a daughter of one of her students, and I drifted over to eavesdrop. The girl's father's name, she said, was Raphael Poño, pronounced in the Filipino style, with a hard "r" and soft "n." No, no, the teacher said, demonstrating how to say "Raphael Poño" with meticulous, Spanish classroom care. This is how it's pronounced, she said.

That was a long time ago, and she was young. Maybe, if she's gone on to have the career she'd planned, some of her edges have been knocked off and she's learned that other people have things to teach her. But her case illustrates some of the perils of plunging into ambition for righteousness, however well-intentioned. We don't always know what righteousness is, and we get things wrong with dismal ease. Before we go conceiving ambition about enacting a good life, lived for God, we should spend some time asking what goodness is, and what God might want from us. If we are on fire with ambition, rearing to do things for our Lord, and we discover that our Lord's desire for us is to live a quiet, suburban life whose only grandeur comes in acts of kindness we're occasionally able to offer neighbors who are more or less indifferent to our attempts, will our ambitions be satisfied?

Maybe the best service that ambition can provide is in showing us the never-ending unwieldiness of our egos.

⌁

I once had a student who was particularly ambitious. Even her friends called her a hustler, and it was hard to miss the uneasy judgment in their voices. There was no situation that didn't have a commercial angle to be scrutinized, no relationship that couldn't be turned to great career profit. I liked her; she was brash and interesting, and I liked to make her laugh. But I always kept a slightly wary eye on her, too.

I sometimes mention in class that I have worked out a theology of daily living, and that anyone who wants to hear about it is welcome to ask. The only one to take up my offer that year, interestingly, was this woman, strolling into my office one day between classes. So I told her.

Our daily life, I said, is as close as I've come to an understanding of the crucifixion, and we reenact it every day. Every day, responding to the people we love and the ones we don't, we work to the furthest extent of our talent and intelligence, trying to meet our obligations and at the same time creating something lasting and important. When we're on our game, we pour every good energy we have into the work, and to do that leaves us vulnerable and exposed, in a posture of complete openness. Like someone hanging on a cross.

And then? And then people walk past. One or two might look up and notice us there, writhing and unable to protect ourselves; the rest are busy with their own lives, and don't see. The next day, we do this again. The next, again. For the rest of our lives, our ambition leaves us defenseless against the indifference and sometimes the cruelty of the world. If you're not okay with that, best to find another day job.

Her eyes narrowed, and she looked at the crummy carpet in my office. "Do you understand?" I said.

"I thought you were going to tell a joke," she said.

❧

Writing this essay is not calling forth my best self. I've snapped at my husband and my dogs, who didn't do anything wrong, and this morning I was impatient with my mother, who was trying to make sense of her bank statement. My brother and I have taken most financial responsibility away from her, but she still pores over her monthly statements, trying to remember what the words and numbers mean. I'm trying to get the monthly statements stopped, too.

"Just send it to me," I say. "Don't even open it. I'll take care of anything that needs attention."

I can hear her frowning at the statement. "I should be able to do this."

"I'll take care of it for you." I hear her sigh, and soften my tone. "Why don't you put it away until tomorrow? Maybe it will be easier for you then." She may have dementia, but she isn't an idiot. She knows a lie when she hears one. But she's also kind, and she loves me, and she doesn't take a swipe at me even though I've earned one. She does call again in the after-noon, though.

This time her voice is ragged from tears. "It doesn't make sense! But it shouldn't be hard. I've done this all my life. I don't want you to see what I've done to my—" her voice falters. She means "check record," but can't remember the phrase.

"I've made a decision, and I want you to help me," she says. "I want to look over my will. I can't remember what's there, and that's terrible. I want to get a copy of it."

"We can do that," I tell her. We can. We've done it twice before.

"I'm going to take notes," she says. "That will help. I don't want to forget things anymore."

<p>

The blockbuster novel that became an award-winning movie. The last ten pounds, now twelve. French. Kant. Scuba diving. Keats's "To Autumn." A single day of compassion for all living things.

On the other side of the ledger? One word choice so precise and clear it still makes my heart lift. The friend who said, "I never would have gotten through this without you." The decent French accent. No matter how much I whine, I don't achieve nothing. I just don't achieve the things I think I should.

I witness this in miniature every morning as I set out to do good, use-ful, necessary things in prayer, things that any ambition would be proud to claim. There is the long list of family, friends, and friends of friends calling for intercession. There are the great needs of the world. There is gratitude. There is apology. Sometimes I feel a particular rush of warmth with one or another of these little tasks checked off my prayer to-do list, convincing me that God is listening, and that God and I are really talking to each other. More often, I dully work down the list.

Sometimes, though, I'll be distracted by bird song or the sigh of my dog, or by a warm, pulsing sense of well-being. It's the kind of moment that would make a person, if she was paying attention, glad to have a body to hear and feel with. If that person thought a little more, she might feel God's intent pulling her away from her diligent prayer, even though the prayer has such excellent ambitions. God can't possibly want her just to sit there and feel inexpressibly good. Nothing can be gained from that. If the person gives in, though, and listens to the cardinal's song and the contented, steady breaths of a comfortable dog, and feels her own heart rise for no earthly reason at all, the person might feel a moment of utter, contented joy.

After a while she can get up and on with things. There's work to be done.

2

What I Learned in Lent

Luci Shaw

IN A *NEW YORKER* article I read, back in 2008, John Adams is quoted as having written in his diary in 1759, "I feel anxious, eager, after something. What is it?" It was the same thing it always was: the pain of insatiable ambition. "I have a dread of Contempt, a quick sense of Neglect, a strong Desire of Distinction."

In a similar vein, in the same magazine, writer Louis Menand comments on Arthur Schlesinger who, he says, "liked being liked much more than he disliked being disliked, and his greatest happiness was the recognition of his fellow-establishmentarians."

Katherine Hepburn wrote candidly: "I was ambitious and knew I would not have children. I wanted total freedom."

Then there was Barry Bonds and his comment on the Cable News Network about his alleged use of performance-enhancing drugs: "Athletes are trained and conditioned to want to be Number One. Everything in their lives is motivated by that ambition."

A more recent *New Yorker* cartoon showed two old men in conversation. One says to the other: "I aspired to authenticity, but I never got beyond verisimilitude."

A far more ancient testimony reveals this common human urge: "The scribes and Pharisees . . . do all their deeds to be seen by others, for they make their phylacteries broad and their fringes long. They love to have the place of honor at banquets and the best seats in the synagogues, and to be greeted with respect in the marketplaces and to have people call them rabbi. . . . All who exalt themselves will be humbled, and all who humble themselves will be exalted" (Matt 23:2, 5–7, 12 NRSV).

◞

In a culture where it is generally believed that just about anyone can fulfill their dreams and achieve success, ambition is most often viewed as a positive character attribute. A web site lists quotations about ambition that will "inspire, empower and motivate you to live the life of your dreams and become the person you've always wanted to be!"

For my own recent Lenten reflection, I began to ponder the place of ambition and the desire for recognition in my own life, the life of a Christian who is a writer. Early on in my writing years, with five children and a publisher husband as well as all the tasks of a young, thriving publishing house to tend to (for me this included editorial supervision, book design, and production as well as "author relations"—a large responsibility), my own writing had to come in the crevices between many other things. Yet it persisted. I couldn't not write. The need to translate experience into poetry and commentary kept inserting its head into the cracks. I'd write at night when the kids were asleep. Out walking in the Illinois prairie where we lived, I'd adapt my rhythm to iambic pentameter as I observed the grassy verges of the hiking paths and the changes brought on by seasons. Lines of poetry took shape in my head to be jotted down in my journal as soon as I got home. I even bought a little recording machine, a novelty in those days, to speak into, to talk to so the words wouldn't vanish. I was possessed by poetry, by language and its music.

At the beginning the motivation was pure—a powerful desire to alert others to what I was seeing that they might have missed but that shouldn't be ignored. A sense that this was a gift to be shared, a God-given ability that I was to "stir up" if I was to fulfill a divine purpose for me. I was a very earnest Christian with a conservative church life. I took seriously the idea of a calling. Even though I was a woman. (In those days, in that church, men were supremely dominant and women knew their place, which was to keep quiet and avoid intellectual questions or leanings or, heaven help us, ideas.)

Time passed. I kept writing and sending out my poems, and they began to appear in a few magazines. I sensed early on that these periodicals, by definition, came and went; I might have readers for a month or so, until the next month's issue was published. And then my poem could end up in some landfill.

I realized I didn't want to be a magazine, a disposable trifle. I wanted to be a book. I wanted a long and eloquent life on someone's bookshelf.

The kids grew alongside all the trials and triumphs of my maternal life. My first book, *Listen to the Green*, a gathering of poems with a sweet cover photo of a grass stem holding a drop of dew, appeared in print. This was before self-publishing had gained much traction or respect. People murmured about the fact that our own publishing company published it: "Harold has to publish her book. He's married to her." But the book did capture attention. In the Christian community of that time it was something of an oddity. Poetry wasn't the language most of my people were used to talking. Or reading.

Harold and I determined to do something about it. We established a series of poetry collections and literary biographies to supplement the Bible study guides and devotional books that we called "tools for the thoughtful Christian."

In 1986, I lost Harold to lung cancer, husband of thirty-three years, best friend and advocate. Life changed radically. I became president of Shaw Publishers with the responsibilities of leadership. I had a seasoned and competent staff. We worked well together and the company flourished. But after several years, heading up a business, even with skilled help, became burdensome for me, and I sold our publishing enterprise to Random House/Waterbrook.

As I kept on with my own writing, my world expanded with an enlarging circle of friends and writers, and my poetry began to find more and more outlets.

In terms of achieving a readership, I made a conscious determination to follow rather than seek opportunities to write, speak, and teach. I had my mother's stern admonitions about humility well ingrained. But I remember the euphoria, momentary but dizzying, when from time to time my work appeared in print, and I began to get happy letters from readers and editors.

This encouragement spurred me on, and almost without noticing it, I think my motivation shifted. I'd tasted, and relished, and thereafter yearned for, needed, longed for the ongoing affirmation of publication and positive reviews. It was what kept me going in a time of learning to live on my own. Yet when my collection *Polishing the Petoskey Stone* came out and the finished book was in my hands, there was a distinct sense of anticlimax. Here was this thing, this physical object. What was I to do next but start writing again, compiling another assortment of poetry for publication and hoping for wider circulation?

↤↦

Is ambition the rogue child of ego? Here I'm using ego not in the technical, Freudian sense, but more in reference to that part of each of us that craves identity, recognition, affirmation, and attention. We may write or paint or sculpt out of our own feelings of inadequacy and woundedness, hoping for healing. We may trust that what we write or make of experience will be worth viewing, will contribute to others' understanding. Our ambition may reflect a longing that we'll produce something different from anything else in the world; that as it grows, our work will be recognized as special, even unique; that it will make a difference, communicating the beautiful, the meaningful, the eye-opening, in a lasting way. The way begins to open up and we follow it fervently.

Henri Nouwen's classic, *The Genesee Diary*, a narrative of his seven-month stay in a contemplative monastic community, speaks to our human obsession to be noticed. He said: "Solitude is really hard when you realize that no one is thinking about you." This was a hard lesson for him, but he came to realize the value of our sameness, our anonymity, because it was in Jesus's "sameness" with humanity that God gave Him His unique name and character as the Divine/human link between heaven and earth. He was commissioned to proclaim His identity as God incarnate.

And for me, self-promotion has always felt ungodly, self-indulgent, and a bit pathetic. It is also exhausting.

Do any of us contest the reality of the urge for recognition? I know I cannot. I found some definitions: Ambition (noun): "An ardent desire for distinction." Ambitious (adjective): "Rising, swelling, towering, surrounding."

Yes, I said to myself. I know.

↤↦

It may be that our ambition for excellence is in service to the very practical aspects of our lives: the need to make a living and support a family. My academic tenure may depend on my productivity; unless I write and publish, my contract may not be renewed. Or, I'm doing research that has revealed something that may be beneficial, even vital, for human welfare, something that needs to be made known.

But then I ask myself: "How does ambition differ from vision and vocation?" Frederick Buechner famously wrote that "the place God calls you to is the place where your deep gladness and the world's deep hunger meet." But it's not just the world's deep need that I feel. It's my own personal, desperate need as an individual to be a physical, soulful presence in the world.

When what we are passionately writing about plucks a chord in our readers, it may be a sign that God is in it. Our vocation will often have a deep spiritual source: we may feel the Divine hand in the opportunities that come our way and beckon us. In the ideas, images, and connections that float into our imaginations and cloak themselves in words and phrases in our journals, our computer screens, we may acknowledge our source, God's Spirit.

Obedience
When my fingers
know better than I
as they hover over
the keyboard, then type
a word that is not
the word I wanted but
a better word—what is that
but an answer. You
caring for details, filling
cracks, your tongue
arc-ing its swift current
through my bones.

❧

Perhaps it is our motivation, our purpose that is at the heart of the distinction. Our vision may very well rise from our relationship with the culture around us and our desire to enrich it, challenge it, or redirect it in some way. Madeleine L'Engle viewed such contributions to our human community as "feeding the lake," the same way springs and streams from surrounding hillsides join and form a body of water from which all may drink and be refreshed. Maybe even transformed. What kind of a trickle am I? Am I sparkling and pure, or murky and polluted? Do I want to be recognized for my contribution, or am I content to have a larger, more generous purpose? I'm investigating my own life here. These are issues I continue to wrestle with.

Ambition often involves competition. An etymological dictionary suggests that to compete means "to run with, to run along-side with others" (com = with, and ped = feet). I love this idea! I have company. I'm not alone.

I remember a conversation with Al Young, at that time the Poet Laureate of California, to whom I once confessed my frustration at being "too literary for the Christian market and too Christian for the literary market." He was thoughtful for a moment and then advised me: "If I were you, I'd just scatter your seed wherever it finds fertile ground. Your readers will find you."

And it seems I have been given a readership among people of faith, and although now that it's edging out into the mainstream literary world, my call is still to show that poetry by a Christian need not be saccharine, sentimental, sanctimonious, shallow. So now my ambition has been shaped and nudged into a particular setting, and my ardent wish is that it will fulfill its mission there in ways over which I have little control except to be available and to keep writing.

Yet fame is an addictive drug. No matter how much acclaim an artist or writer receives, it never feels quite enough. The satisfaction gained is short-lived; all too soon the warm feeling of gratification wears off, the happiness is hollow. There are an increasing number of gifted writers vying for a space in the literary world. It is a highly competitive arena, and a continuing series of successful books or gallery showings or performances or lectures is needed to recapture the attention of a fickle audience. There's a very precarious balance between over-confidence and self-doubt. And social networking only complicates things.

Sometimes *Schadenfreude* kicks in. I heard a smug, rather evil quote from another writer, "The books of my colleague have been remaindered!" (Read: "If someone is experiencing a lack of success, perhaps that means I'm getting ahead.")

I think of Annie Dillard, winning the Pulitizer Prize for General Nonfiction in her twenties for *Pilgrim at Tinker Creek*. After that, what was left for her to do? She once complained to me that the books she has written since are "little, little books." This makes my admiration for a writer like Marilynne Robinson all the greater. She took ten years after the publication of *Housekeeping* to write her Pulitzer prize-winning, grace-filled novel, *Gilead*, and was deliberate in the slow development of its companion *Home*— same characters, different narrator—that mirrored the theme of gradually and deeply-formed relationships.

Celebrity and fame, the bastard offsprings of unfettered ambition, often come at a cost to soul and spirit health. Hardly noticing the transition, we may find that pursuing our own career has become the driving force, the deity in our lives. It's a form of idolatry that comes almost imperceptibly, but as the addiction grows, consuming us with our self-importance, it may morph into greed, one of the seven deadly sins. The resulting soul-erosion can be toxic and devastating. We may become cultural icons, heroes, celebrities, but our souls are shriveled within us.

Poet Dana Gioia talks about his years as chairman of the National Endowment for the Arts in Washington, DC, and the power structures he observed in every part of government, not just politics. He thinks that such access to power has become a corrupting addiction, a disease that is difficult to treat because it is rarely acknowledged and has become so widespread and state-of-the-art.

My own life-long sense of inadequacy; I was a firstborn, a girl, but in our British family the son, my younger brother, was the heir who received the bounty of inheritance, leadership, and significance. My parents loved me, but though I strove to please them, it was never enough. Any form of "vanity" was systematically squeezed out of me. My mother's greatest fear was that I would become proud. Since then my instinctive response to any success has been that it was an accident, undeserved. As the prophet Samuel asked, "Who am I, O Lord God, . . . that you have brought me thus far?" (2 Sam 7:18 NRSV).

I tend to swing back and forth between self-congratulation and doubt about my work, like a pair of sneakers swaying as they hang from a telephone wire, laces dangling.

So there's a tension between a covenant with God in which we offer Him ourselves and our gifts for His purposes, and our tendency to take the credit for our accomplishments. So much hard work and persistence has been invested in our book, our new art piece, our music. We've struggled for so long to polish and focus our gift. "Surely," we find ourselves thinking, "we deserve some acknowledgment!"

Other questions for reflection come to mind. Because our sense of self is easily wounded, especially if we are hypersensitive artists, we crave a comforting recognition, a gratifying place on center stage.

So I ask myself, "What parts do elements of self-esteem and self-confidence play in my growth and productivity? Is it my need for recognition that drives me? What is my primary calling, my passion, my vision? Can my ego drive—to move ahead and make a name for myself—lead to an obsession or reflect a growing narcissism?"

Last year I read a review of a new book, *Dangerous Ambition: Women in Search of Love and Power*, about Rebecca West and Dorothy Thompson, two career women writers who gained prominence in the 1930s. The reviewer tells us that the book is "a study of female emancipation and literary culture, and an acute analysis of dysfunctional family life." Of their children it was noted that, "resentful of their mothers after lonely childhoods, both sons married young, abandoned their wives, pursued unrealistic ambitions that proved unsuccessful, and demanded lifelong financial assistance." A family horror story of ambition gone wrong.

We are familiar with the phrase "overweening ambition." What is it that leads to this extreme? Does my desire to do my best and share my work with an audience constitute ambition or faithfulness to my calling? Are my aspirations for excellence misguided? Are there benefits—emotional or spiritual—to being humble or self-effacing? To what extent does my view of myself depend on the opinions of others? My character and my integrity may be threatened or eroded by growing celebrity and fame, but are there positive statements to be made about ambition?

In the competitive world of Western culture these questions seem to be of particular significance. Without a modicum of self-promotion—"marketing oneself"—how will a struggling poet or a beginning but promising artist, writer, or musician be in a position to contribute to the world of ideas, images, attitudes, and ethics that shape our culture? What wisdom can we gain from leaders who have achieved a name for themselves through their work? How have they dealt with (or not dealt with) the enticements of fame and the perks and privileges of public life? My friend, the singer Karin Bergquist, has a tattoo: "Comparisons are the thief of joy."

And the wise Wendell Berry wrote: "The individual always has two ways to turn: she or he may turn either toward the household and community, to receive membership and to give service, or toward the relatively unconditional life of the public, in which one is free to pursue self-realization, self-aggrandizement, self-interest, self-fulfillment, self-enrichment, self-promotion, and so on."

Yet our human propensity for pride, independent action, and resulting power has been getting us in trouble since the dawn of history. It is at the root of many human woes, not the least of which is the egregious desire to take credit for things that go right in our lives and to blame God for things that go wrong. I believe that the term "gifted writer," "gifted artist," "gifted musician," or "gifted scientist" refers not only to what has been given us—what has called us insistently into an enthusiasm, a way of life, a refining of our communicative skills—but to what we have been given to give, even to give away. A surplus of fame may lead to objectification. No thoughtful person wants to be famous for being famous. Pedestals provide targets, opportunities for being tumbled to the ground.

When Donald Hall, the acclaimed, profoundly gifted American poet, was asked at a literature conference what place ambition had in his life, he responded, "Ambition? Forget about it. Get over it as fast as you can. If I have any ambition it is for my work, not for myself." After hearing this response and reading Hall's seminal book, *On Poetry and Ambition*, I came to realize that success and acclaim do not nullify the validity of ambition, which should be on behalf of what we create rather than to boost our egos. His conviction is that an artist's or writer's life work is to communicate insights, experience, wisdom, and truth in the written or unwritten word, rather than to seek personal acclaim or fame.

It's ironic, however, that because acclaim clung to him, in his memoir *Unpacking the Boxes,* he couldn't resist the temptation of egregious name-dropping and offering a long list of his well-publicized literary accomplishments and awards. It's as if his own moral philosophy had been eroded by his need to be known and acclaimed. His personal rationalization: "Ambition exists to provide a venue for the libido," and "In the absence of athletic skill, I found that poetry attracted at least the arty girls if not the cheerleaders." Which doesn't elevate him above his own pretensions.

Yet it was Hall's earlier comment that triggered my thoughts and questions about the place of ambition in the life of individuals in the public sphere as well as those at the beginning of a career. A common but infrequently addressed tension could be summed up in the question, "Is it OK to be ambitious?" This tension moves through every aspect of life, vocation, avocation, and "the American dream" with special appeal to those who, with integrity, seek to develop their life potential as a gift from God. St. Paul wrote to his young colleague Timothy, telling him to "kindle afresh the gift that is in you" (2 Tim 1:6 NASV). Our double responsibility is to be faithful to both gift and Giver. Accountability is handed to us along with the gift.

I once heard poet and biographer Paul Mariani comment in an almost offhand way to a group: "Your gift is your spiritual discipline." I pursued this thought and concluded that if any of us have received a certain ability, an aptitude for a specific role in life, it is there to be nourished and shared with others. It has a reason for being.

I find this refreshing and reassuring. I am not particularly good at disciplined Bible reading or study, or reading the Daily Office, though my life has been constantly nudged in that direction. I find liturgy nourishing. But writing is what brings me a spiritual and even physical joy and sense of the Spirit's active work in me that convinces me that I'm being responsible to God. I like what Benjamin Disraeli said: "The secret of success is constancy to purpose."

Our double responsibility is to be faithful to both gift and Giver. Accountability comes with the gift. The Christ in me has no need of fame, celebrity, acclaim. Remember, "He humbled himself . . ."? St. Paul tells us to "think of yourselves the way Christ Jesus thought of himself. He had equal status with God but didn't think so much of himself that he had to cling to the advantages of status . . . He didn't claim special privileges. Instead, he lived a selfless, obedient life and then died a selfless, obedient death . . . Because of that obedience God lifted him high and honored him far beyond anyone or anything" (Phil 2:3–11, THE MESSAGE). "Blessed are the poor in spirit," Jesus, told the crowd in the Beatitudes, the blessings (Matt 5:3 NRSV).

"Godliness with contentment is great gain" (1 Tim 6:6 KJV). (Someone called this "the rich simplicity of being yourself before God.")

My Wheaton College professor, mentor, and friend, Clyde Kilby, once gave me a small book by Brewster Ghiselin, *The Creative Process*, with a number of essays that suggest that the seminal ideas, the brilliant hunches, the "Eureka moments" of scientists, philosophers, writers, inventors come from somewhere beyond human beings. They are unanticipated gifts from "God knows where." I take that quite literally. As I pay attention to the messages of the universe, my well-honed and receptive imagination is enabled to play with a plenitude of images and connections that arrive from beyond me, provided by a Creator whose gifts encourage me to create.

Phrases fly at me through space like insects to be caught in the filaments of the mind. Colors and textures evoke their psychic counterparts.
My job is to be open, to attend and allow that enlarging vortex of ideas to
expand, and then to nudge them into a form. It's as if the Genesis creation
story is happening over and over again in a small, deeply individual way.

The artist's dilemma is that they may find themselves forging ahead
into an often indifferent world to offer what they have to share. To continue
to move ahead with conviction demands persistence and a degree of courage and confidence in the worth of the gift. Sometimes we need outside
encouragement to assure us that our gifts really have value. This is where
good critical assessment from teachers or colleagues is invaluable. I regularly "workshop" developing writing with friends whose opinions I value
and who can often detect flaws in my new work that I am too besotted with
it to notice.

⌘

I wonder about the decisions of G. M. Hopkins who never saw any of his
poetry published during his lifetime. It was only years after his death that
his friend Robert Bridges, in 1917, pulled together what he had gathered
through correspondence with Hopkins into a publishable body of work.
Today, in the library of Trinity College, Dublin, many stacks of apprecia-
tive critical work about Hopkins's oeuvre fill the shelves. The worldwide
acknowledgment of Hopkins as one of the greatest metaphysical poets
increases.

As I read Paul Mariani's exhaustive biography, *Gerard Manley Hopkins: A Life*, I found further clues to Hopkins's vision and motivation, both
for his act of burning his early poems in a personal holocaust he called in
his journal "the slaughter of the innocents," and the moment when, as a
Jesuit priest, he was startled into writing "The Wreck of the Deutschland"
about the death of the nuns who perished when their ship went down and
began again to fulfill his poetic vocation. He wanted nothing, not even his
creative gifts, to impede his desire to serve God.

The word that is pressed in on me again and again is humility—not
a gift that is easy for me to accept and practice. It goes against my human
grain. Yet a slew of biblical comments let me know what God looks for and
blesses: He "opposes the proud but gives grace to the humble" (Prov 3:34;
Jas 4:6 KJV). In the New Testament Peter quotes this same Old Testament

injunction, "Clothe yourselves with humility in your dealings with one another, for God opposes the proud but gives grace to the humble" (1 Pet 5:6 KJV).

Self-proclaimed humility is, of course, an oxymoron, so perhaps it is better to come at it from its opposite, hubris—presumption, pride, excessive self-confidence. Might deliberate, conscious shunning of hubris bring about a work of grace in us, bring us into line—a fine balance between self-abnegation and arrogance? Can remaining in anonymity—one small individual in a "cloud of witnesses"—be preferred to taking on the treacherous role of achieving fame and prominence?

James Watson continues to be celebrated for the discovery of the double helix (the structure of chromosomal strands of nucleic acid such as RNA and DNA), a major scientific breakthrough that won him the Nobel Prize. In 1968, Watson wrote a book celebrating his own role while downplaying the major contributions of his colleagues, Francis Crick, Maurice Wilkins, and Rosalind Franklin. While Watson feasted on the limelight and grabbed the headlines, Crick commented that he was simply grateful to have helped provide the world with this scientific advance. Crick's response shows me the kind of reaction I'd like to see in myself.

I also find encouragement toward humility in the concept of "self-donation" as described in Miroslav Volf's book *Exclusion and Embrace*. For followers of Christ, servanthood, faithfulness to one's calling whether recognized or not, and the example of Jesus's *kenosis*, a self-emptying as described in Philippians 2, speaks of the values God honors. I ask myself, "Is God honoring me for my small contribution or am I taking all the credit for myself?"

Reviewing the ways I seem to be viewed by others all seems so central to my identity and cannot be denied. But to count on them in order to feel approved of and gratified can foster hubris. My most significant entry into my résumé, my most valued biographical relationship, is with my Creator.

Pride is a besetting sin, one of the seven deadlies. As C. S. Lewis observed, "Pride is a kind of soul cancer." It all started with the independence of Eden. In our own day it has been turned on its head and presented as a self-satisfied expression of our identity: "I'm proud to be an American and represent my country on the Olympic team." "I'm proud of my political affiliation." "I'm proud of my seventh grader and her high grades."

There is a skin condition known as "proud flesh"—an excessive accumulation of "granular tissue" or normal tissue that has become "overactive." Proud flesh can also apply to the spirit.

And pride comes before a fall. We see this in politicians who have taken advantage of their power, become corrupt by accepting bribes from lobbyists only to be exposed and demoted. By contrast, the prophet Micah enjoins us "to walk humbly with thy God" (Micah 6:8 KJV). In the epistle of James, Christians are instructed to "humble yourselves in the sight of the Lord and he will lift you up" (4:10 KJV). We long to be lifted up. We need to know that God supervises the process and our part may be to start at the bottom.

I like the derivation of the words humble and humility. They come from the same root as humus, the earthy substance that is formed from the death and decay of organic matter, a substrate that provides a kind of culture or growth medium for new life and development. We do this in our own backyard, in a compost bin into which we deposit the slimy lettuce, potato peelings, rotten fruit, etc., which have sat too long in the refrigerator. It provides the busy worm population in the bin with a fecund source of nutrition. Come spring, we spread this rich mix in our garden and the result is fertility, green and colorful growth. The word human comes from the same source.

We need to reflect on these words if we are to understand how our God sees us and what He desires for us under His supervision.

⊖

Reading *Copenhagen*, an intriguing play by Michael Frayn about a puzzling and unexplained visit that physicist Werner Heisenberg made to Niels Bohr in Denmark during World War II, I learned something about observation of subatomic particles and what has been called "the uncertainty principle." According to Frayn, this principle discovered and articulated by Erwin Schrondinger, in the context of the impossibility of quantitative observation of electrons, can be applied in a totally different sphere—the understanding of our own souls, minds, and motives. It is almost impossible for us to examine ourselves dispassionately, objectively.

Frayn, in his epilogue, describes the research that went into the writing of the play, remarking, "One's thoughts and intentions, perhaps one's own most of all, remain shifting and elusive. There is not one single thought or intention of any sort that can ever be precisely established." Self-consciousness, self-analysis creeps in whenever we try to assess our own state of mind, muddying our conclusions.

Ideas, images, words, and tunes circle the brain like scatters of leaves in a gust of wind. Things shift and slip and reshape themselves during the mental process of self-examination. In the very act of introspection we put our own motives and thoughts to flight, the way subatomic particles shift in the very act of scientific observation. We realize how easy it is to deceive ourselves especially when we are looking for justification. Our rationalizations are tainted by even thinking about them.

Most of us would readily admit to thoroughly mixed motivations for the projects that seem to be of greatest importance to us. Even though we attempt to be honest and sincere, the search for the self within the self may easily slip past reality into morbid introspection or self-justification, unless it ends up striking through to our heart of hearts and discovers God is there all along.

We need an Eye, an Ear, a Touch beyond ourselves. Candid critique has its benefits but in the end human seeing or listening is inadequate. Our most intimate friends, colleagues, spouses, even our spiritual mentors or therapists, may be deceived or make wrong assumptions about our inner lives.

It's not that we lack the skills and abilities to do good work. We may be gifted, competent, creative. We want to learn as we go, and in our mature years we hope to have gained wisdom and genuineness. Like comets, we may trail behind us a plume of work well done, writing or art that seems to justify its existence. We need to ask (without knowing the answer): What is its eternal value? Was it done to God's glory? When we invite God into every task, seek wisdom, trust the help that comes with prayer, the work itself becomes a sacrament. The immediate and the infinite join hands.

My prayer today and for the future is this:

> O Lord, you have searched me and known me.
> You know when I sit down and when I rise up;
> you discern my thoughts from far away.
> You search out my path and my lying down,

and are acquainted with all my ways.
Even before a word is on my tongue,
   O Lord, you know it completely.
Search me, O God, and know my heart;
   test me and know my thoughts;
See if there is any wicked way in me,
   and lead me in the way everlasting.
—Ps 139:1–4, 23–24 NRSV

3

The Lure of Fame

The Yearning, the Drive, the Question Mark

Emilie Griffin

WHEN I WAS YOUNG I fell in love with Fame. I yearned with a real intensity for recognition, achievement, reward. The yearning began when I was in middle school and high school. At seventeen, when I entered college, the question of fame filled my thoughts. I was young, my whole life was in front of me; I had no idea what the future held or what I could aspire to, yet I felt sure that Fame was in store. By "Fame" I meant celebrity, notoriety, being known or recognized for something. Winning a Fulbright scholarship. Gaining the English prize. Winning a writing contest. Getting singled out or honored for high achievement. Recognition of some kind. Maybe I didn't care what kind. I just imagined being center stage, taking extra bows, being weighed down with roses like a *prima donna*, flooded in a spotlight blaze of glory. Stardom was totally appealing.

Notice that I have capitalized the word "Fame." In those days and probably since, Fame was a kind of goddess. I wanted Fame, and I was afraid of her. She was a banshee on the road, luring me. Like the will o' the wisp of Irish lore, she exerted quite a fascination. But that very attraction frightened me. Milton's words influenced me then:

> Fame is the spur that the clear spirit doth raise
> That last infirmity of noble mind.

Milton seemed to think that his own desire for Fame was a weakness, a danger point in his drive to write great poetry and to measure up to his high gifts. Perhaps he also felt a sense of obligation for his years of reading and scholarship. Others, especially his father, had sacrificed to make that possible for him.

Did I really fall in love with Fame? Was I seduced by the idea of becoming famous? Was celebrity or notoriety my dream? Or was I simply exploring the boundaries of existence, as young people are meant to do? Was it a real temptation of sorts? Or just an exaggerated fear, a lack of confidence? I'm not entirely sure.

In this same period I had another obsession. I wanted desperately to fall in love, to climb the heights of human experience. I imagined a kind of fulfillment or completion that love, that is to say romantic love, would provide. For some reason I saw these as competing objectives. Falling in love with a person, I sensed, might prevent me from pursuing a higher life dream.

There was another wrinkle in my thought as I played with these ideas, for playing it was. I was examining, exploring the limits of life, my opportunities and boundaries. Possibly I was also afraid of my own intellect, of being a person of high talents and gifts. What was I expected to do with the gifts and talents I had received? How could I live up to my family's expectations, and my own? And then there was the question of God. What did God, who I suspected had bestowed the gifts in the first place, expect of me?

During the years I speak of—high school and college—I was under the spell of some great classical writers. I was reading Shakespeare, Milton, and the nineteenth-century British poets. Many of them were writing about the lure of ambition, the dangers of a desire for fame. I had memorized, and even performed, the great speeches in *Julius Caesar* about Caesar's desire for fame and glory. In Shakespeare's play, these words are delivered by Mark Antony after Caesar has been assassinated.

> When that the poor have cried, Caesar hath wept,
> Ambition should be made of sterner stuff.
> Yet Brutus says he was ambitious.
> And Brutus is an honorable man.

At the same time I was studying the ancient world, especially the Latin essayists and poets, Cicero and Horace, Ovid and Catullus, the satirists, the playwrights, the writers of epigrams. Every one of them seemed to touch on my great themes: ambition and the desire for fame, and the pitfalls of romantic love. Maybe it wasn't a real dilemma but I definitely thought it was.

Yet this quest of mine seemed somewhat ordinary at the time. Students signed up for classes. We attended lectures and read the assigned texts more or less attentively. Some of us talked about and pondered the big ideas. Was Aristotle right about the meaning of things? Or did Plato have the better argument? What was the proper place of the artist in society? What should one give one's life to? What did Judaism have to say on the subject? What about the Christian claims, the radical claims of Jesus Christ? What about the Law and the Prophets? What about the biblical insistence on generosity and love?

I remember how much I identified with Milton's life quest. He had invested everything in the dream of becoming not just a poet, but one of the great poets of all time. He fretted that he had not achieved very much by the time he had reached the exalted age of twenty-three. Admittedly, manhood came sooner in Milton's time. But Milton was anxious, and about the same things that bothered me. He did not worry so much about the challenge of his contemporaries, as he considered his ultimate place in the larger universe of Homer and Virgil and Dante. These great poets of earlier centuries were his teachers, and in a sense his rivals, for the laurel of high achievement in the life of poetry. I was wrestling with all that. In a high school discussion I had heard one of my classmates say, "I just want to find my place in the universe." As silly as it sounded, that was my objective too.

On a more practical level I was conscious of the sacrifices my mother had made—she was a single parent and a working mother—to secure the best kind of education for me. What did I owe her for the advantages she had given me? She kept saying her personal sacrifices didn't matter, but I felt, more on some days than others, that she had a dream for my life, one that I didn't fully understand, not my dream but hers, and I didn't know exactly what I should do about it, how I should proceed, what choices I should make.

In retrospect I think it was a time of profound self-discovery. Psychologists would no doubt call it identity development. Philosophers might speak about the quest for truth. For me it was both, and a religious quest as well. I was looking for someone or something that would make my life complete. Ultimately, I learned that the destination and the yearning was for God—God in Jesus Christ, God in His full Trinitarian beauty, transcendence, and humanity. Human love was part of that, a reflection of Divine love, but God was All in All.

Now I see that the question of Fame was more than a youthful quest. Today, many decades later, the question remains. Is it all right to want Fame? What's the difference between legitimate aspiration and drive, and a competitive impulse that is out of control?

⌁

What's wrong with wanting fame?

Probably the best answer to this prickly question came to me first in a popular song:

> Fame, if you win it,
>
> Comes and goes in a minute.
>
> Where's the real stuff in life to cling to?

Whenever I hear those lyrics I also hear the crackly sound of Jimmy Durante's voice, since he was one entertainer who popularized that song. The words are humorous and light, but I think the message is sound.

⌁

Fame is not only fleeting and uncertain. It is truly a false and delusionary dream.

Ambition—now, that's all right. Or is it?

Aren't both fame and ambition false dreams—because they are elusive, because we risk everything for them and they ultimately let us down?

In the life of the creative artist this issue is critical. Often, in order to write an extended work—a novel, a film, a play—the creative artist makes some radical sacrifice. He or she may decide against a high-paying job in order to move to a remote cabin in the woods and write. Or else the aspiring writer takes a job as a creative writing teacher when a more lucrative opportunity beckons. Sometimes a writer relies on the income and diligence of a spouse, dreaming of a movie sale, bestseller status, a big financial reward that never materializes. No doubt the same issue applies in other professions: building the great corporation, the outstanding law firm, making the long-range commitment needed for a great scientific discovery. What are we dreaming of? What are we doing it for?

↶

Examining a life

"The unexamined life is not worth living," Aristotle wrote. His observation is essential, profound, and time-tested. I decided, as I wrestled with the issue of fame, to stop examining my own life (which was in itself a fairly confusing endeavor) and look at a few other notable lives. I chose people who had gained celebrity or fame. Then I refined my search. I decided to examine those who achieved fame and lost it, or felt betrayed by it. I looked for people who had taken the fall pretty hard, and felt that Fame had somehow cheated them. I examined their lives because I thought they might give me a clue to my own.

People in the entertainment field are experts on fame. Actors find their desirability for certain roles has everything to do with celebrity and fame. After years of struggling to become famous, some role of theirs gives them overnight celebrity. Meg Ryan and Julia Roberts are good examples. For me, real enlightenment came when I studied the life of Peter Bowles, a British actor who constantly wrestled with questions of celebrity and success.

Trying to support his family, Peter Bowles was often hard up, struggling to pay the bills. What especially grieved him was that some roles that made him famous (this was true of a long-running television series called *To the Manor Born*) left him unemployable for future parts. His new celebrity "made a name for him" but prevented him from being cast for any other roles for some years. Needless to say, Bowles was wounded and discouraged by this. The "rules of the game" were treacherous. Fame herself had let him down. It was natural to feel a sense of the injustice of things.

In the case of major platform speakers like evangelist Billy Graham, a similar situation prevails. Juggling his commitment to Jesus Christ and his concern for marriage and family, Graham felt totally entranced by the desire for a worldwide ministry. More and more he poured his energies into international travel and evangelistic preaching to huge stadiums full of seekers. The time he could spend at home dwindled. Graham eventually regretted his own attitude and practice. Once, when he failed to recognize his own child on returning home from a long journey, he was full of shame and his conscience wounded him. The child was actually afraid of him, afraid that some stranger was coming to take him away. This incident and others revealed to him that his zeal for God's work had led him to extremes. He felt that he had acted wrongly without fully realizing what was at stake. I'm inclined to think of this as the "lure of the platform." Dr. Graham was a man of conscience who saw the consequences of his style of life, acted honorably, and moved quickly to recover from his own excesses, the ups and downs of celebrity. But others don't fare so well, and sometimes lives and marriages are destroyed by the pressures of celebrity and fame.

Recently the actress Elizabeth Taylor died after a very long life, a number of marriages, and a life of immense wealth and celebrity. I remember how much I admired her beauty and talent when I was young. For men and women in the 1950s she seemed at the pinnacle of achievement. Her films were instantaneous hits. She attracted the hearts and sympathies of millions. At first dismissed as just a pretty starlet, she studied her craft and struggled to take on demanding roles. Taylor wrestled with the extraordinary physical and psychological pressures of stardom, bouncing in and out of hospitals and clinics. She experienced shame and depression, and had to deal with the consequences of her adulteries, her many marriages, and even a condemnation by the Vatican because of her power to influence the young. Taylor and her celebrity husbands were prime examples of the difficulties of fame. Even when she won an Oscar, people ridiculed her for having slept her way to the top. Her life of fame seemed to bring a heavy load of stress and very little consolation. At her death I wondered whether her wealth or stardom ever eased her loneliness. She must have realized that all the success and fame brought her no lasting sense of peace and satisfaction.

This kind of reflecting on the lives of those who achieved great celebrity helped me in my own longing to understand the lure and the delusion of fame.

⟿

The yearning to understand

On reflection, I think that such deep philosophical questions are not resolved in an instant. We get clues and insights at various moments in our lives. Sometimes the answer seems almost within reach. Then the moment of clarity slips away.

One such moment came for me in my early forties, when I was leaving New York, a city where I had lived for twenty years. New York is a city that thrives on celebrity and fame. The life's blood of that city seems to be high achievement and overnight success. In fact, the experience of living in New York—or any notable city—is a lesson in wisdom. Everywhere you turn you find the names of people who once were famous and are now barely remembered. Street names, the names of rivers and tunnels, the names of bridges and skyscrapers, all attest to the fleeting nature of fame. Andy Warhol, the notable artist of the 1960s and '70s, made a memorable remark about everyone achieving "fifteen minutes of fame." I felt sure, when I lived in Queens and Brooklyn and walked to work through Manhattan streets, that Warhol had stretched it a bit. Hardly anyone gets that many minutes. And the celebrity soon fades.

Knowing that we soon would be moving away, I felt compelled to re-visit some places that had been formative to me. I went again to New York art collections and museums that had expanded my vision of the world. I stood in front of the portraits of René Descartes and John Donne in the Frick Collection. I walked into the building on Madison Avenue where the office of *Mademoiselle* magazine had once been. I remembered being a college guest editor there and the number of famous people I had met: Margaret Truman Daniel, the daughter of then President Harry S. Truman, and her husband Clifton Daniel, the editor in chief of the *New York Times*. Actors like Ruth Gordon and Robert Morse. Producers like Jason Robards Jr. and Kermit Bloomgarden. Others I had seen on stage in performances now legendary. Julie Harris and Boris Karloff in Jean Anouilh's lovely play "The Lark." "Where are they now?" I kept thinking, because the world was shifting so fast. I came to realize that that had always been true. When I was young, I thought the generations before me had achieved lasting security and stability. Twenty years later I knew otherwise.

The empress of cold cream

Perhaps the most amazing memory was of Madame Helena Rubinstein. My brief meeting with her was a landmark moment. She was perched on a handsome sofa at one end of a long room, wearing an elaborate Chinese dress and exquisite, embroidered shoes. I guessed she was in her eighties.

She was diminutive. Her feet dangled, almost like a child's, barely touching the floor. She might have been an item in her own collection. Yet her empire, represented by the collection itself, was impressive. Twenty bright young guest editors from *Mademoiselle* had been invited to tour her apartment, a three-story cooperative on Park Avenue. Arriving from a reception where we had feasted on tiny sandwiches and glasses of sherry, we were welcomed at Madame Rubinstein's and went from room to room, viewing her stunning personal collection of art and artifacts. Some were by notable contemporaries, including Salvador Dali and Pablo Picasso. Works by these notables were actually painted on the walls, and signed by the artists themselves: "To my darling Helena from Pablo" and "With affection, Salvador."

As the history of the collection was explained, I realized that the artists in question had not fully known who they were or how famous they and their works would become. Madame Rubinstein, herself an icon, had spent her life in the struggle to build an empire based on cosmetics and cold cream. Everyone—all the actors in this life drama—were driven by a longing to achieve without a sure guarantee of success.

I thought, too, about the life achievement of the guest editors who had been with me that day. Then, we had been young hopefuls, starry-eyed and naïve. Twenty years later, many of us had made names in education, journalism, and the arts. Some had won Pulitzer Prizes and had written notable memoirs. Possibly their names were well-known. Each young woman in that group had her own brush with celebrity and renown. Although their achievements may continue to stand, their high reputations were, well, precarious.

It is all about faith, I thought. It is about a kind of faith that acts in confidence, with a sense of the gift of talent and insight, but without any guarantee of notoriety or fame.

For a moment, my vision was clear.

✵

The need for recognition

Is it the need for recognition that drives me? The sensitive conscience dwells on such things, while others, less introspective, forge ahead to gain a life's dream. To the young poet or beginning artist, I say, "Be of good cheer.

Whether you are young or old, even if you are a middle-aged visionary, don't be discouraged."

If I have any wisdom after more than seventy years of living, and pondering, it is simply this: the drive for recognition is human. It is God's gift to us, and one way that we reflect His glory.

True, the yearning for achievement and recognition is sometimes difficult to manage. Sometimes it goes haywire and puts us totally out of control. Left unchecked, it destroys marriages, corporations, kingdoms, communities, every kind of human enterprise.

But God is with us in our yearning to achieve. It is the Lord God, creator of humanity, who has put this longing in our hearts. Whatever our flawed and stumbling efforts at accomplishment, if our hearts are set toward God, He will transform our feeble attempts into something good.

I take heart from a community of playwrights to which my husband and I belong. Recently, in that community of theatre people, in the humble but high-achieving city of Alexandria, Louisiana, I received a second-place recognition award for a new ten-minute play I had written. My heart surged with happiness. Eight original plays were staged and mine was one of them.

The awards were given, not at Carnegie Hall, not at the Louvre nor the Tuileries Gardens, not at the White House or Versailles. Still, the setting was beautiful. Blue sky and setting sun in our backyard ceremony provided me with all the grandeur I required. In the company of actors, directors, playwrights, and poets, my heart was flooded with happiness. I felt the beauty of the world.

Sure enough, as the production schedule developed, there were dozens of mishaps. Directors were assigned, then disappeared. New directors hurried in to fill the gaps. Actors squabbled over rehearsal times and who would get the best parts. Lines were muffed. Playwrights were cranky about the way their plays were staged. The playwrights' workshop had a few ragged edges and at the last night's performance, one playwright said he had heard complaints that too many of our plays were about God.

As for me, I was glad I had sold about twenty-five tickets at full price and had bought a few really nice T-shirts. They exemplified for me what the artist—through drive and discipline—can contribute to the world. They featured the logo of Spectral Sisters Productions (these are the wicked sisters from Macbeth).

The T-shirts also featured this quote from Oscar Wilde, a man who understood the vagaries of fame. "I regard the theatre as the greatest of all art forms, the most immediate way in which a human being can share with another the sense of what it is to be a human being."

I wore my T-shirt proudly. It was less expensive, perhaps, than Helena Rubinstein's embroidered slippers, but it expressed a bit of my own life dream. I thought Oscar Wilde had it right. It is good to aspire, to deal with the rough and tumble of human enterprise, whatever its vagaries and failings. It is not about fame, celebrity; not for being known for this or that. The competitive urge figures in, with all its human flaws and rivalries. Shakespeare's words, in *Julius Caesar* and elsewhere, offer clues to the lure of fame, the good and bad side of ambition. The ancient world, with its moral imperatives, is with us still, making us hesitate before reaching for power and success. But our drive to succeed aims higher, looks beyond the daily struggle. Ambition should be made of sterner stuff.

The work of our lives is to make the most of our gifts and talents. To share with others the sense of what it is to be a human being. To do this we must be attentive to the yearning we feel to achieve, to contribute, to do well.

4

Ye Shall Be as Gods

Dain Trafton

AMBITION IS A RESTLESS passion. The name comes from the Latin *ambire*: to go about. Those who suffer from ambition must be ever stirring, busy in body and mind to gain power, wealth, and fame. And to hold them tight once won, for the fear of losing them surpasses the fear of never gaining them at all, and they are always threatening to slip away. "The time you won your town the race / We chaired you through the marketplace," writes A. E. Housman. "What have you done today?" we ask.

No one understood ambition's unquiet heart better than Shakespeare, whose portraits of that passion, great and small, tragic and comic, surpass in variety and depth anything that he found in his sources—even in those estimable anatomists of ambition Holinshed and Plutarch.

> Perseverance, dear my lord,
> Keeps honor bright: to have done is to hang
> Quite out of fashion, like a rusty mail
> In monumental mock'ry.

So in *Troilus and Cressida,* the wily Ulysses seeks to lure Achilles back into battle by threatening him with the loss of "honor," which here means fame or reputation, not the deeper, inner quality that men and women in Shakespeare's day sometimes meant. Honor in the sense of fame or reputation is a public matter, which must be burnished in the public eye or lost. What? The "lubber" Ajax or some other upstart steal the credit of killing Hector?

"Take the instant way," Ulysses tells the hero, and baits him with an image of ambition worthy of the *Inferno*:

> For honor travels in a strait so narrow,
>
> Where one but goes abreast. Keep then the path,
>
> For emulation hath a thousand sons
>
> That one by one pursue. If you give way,
>
> Or hedge aside from the direct forthright,
>
> Like to an ent'red tide, they all rush by
>
> And leave you hindmost.

Lasciate ogni speranza, voi ch'entrate (Abandon all hope, you who enter). But Ulysses knows his man. "I see my reputation is at stake, / My fame is shrewdly gor'd," replies Achilles, and in the end he brushes aside his reservations—"Of this my privacy / I have strong reasons"—and like an addict who knows full well the hell to which he goes, embraces it. Not in the hazard of single combat, however, hero against hero as Homer tells the story in the *Iliad*, but in a treacherous ambush. According to Shakespeare, expanding on a hint in Chaucer's *Troilus and Criseyde*, it is not Achilles but his gang of Myrmidons, urged on by their master, who kill Hector while he is alone and unarmed and then, still responding to Achilles' bidding, spread the lie, "Achilles hath the mighty Hector slain," which both camps accept at once: "The bruit is, Hector's slain, and by Achilles." (And might we add that here we see Shakespeare take the instant way to land an ambitious blow on the mighty Homer? And treacherously, great Homer being unable to reply? But that's a story for another essay.)

Like the poor, the ambitious are always with us and always will be, or so we may infer from the book of Genesis, however we read it—literally or metaphorically. In the beginning God gave our first parents a paradise where they could dwell forever in peace and plenty on one condition only: that they not, on pain of death, to eat the fruit of the tree of the knowledge of good and evil. Which prohibition they could not abide, standing as it did between them and the satisfaction of an ambition apparently far more urgent to them than God's commandment or the threat of death. This was an ambition they hardly recognized, much less understood, until the serpent, "more subtle than any beast of the field," deeper than the great Ulysses, perceived it and used it to tempt them: the ambition to "be as gods." "Ye shall not surely die," said the serpent, "For God doth know that in the day ye eat thereof, then your eyes shall be opened, and ye shall be as gods, knowing good and evil." Which bold and utterly implausible assertion, contradicting what they had heard from God, must have resonated deep within our first parents' souls, for Eve, without further inquiry, pausing only to observe with a wonderful stroke of unconscious irony that the forbidden fruit was "to be desired to make one wise," ate, and gave the fruit to Adam, who without a word followed her example (Gen 3 KJV).

Even the angels knew such ambition—some of them at least—for which they lost heaven before Eve and Adam lost paradise, or so a tradition, biblical in origin, of which Milton's *Paradise Lost* is the best-known expression in English, assures us. Of this angelic ambition Satan was the first exponent. It was he who first deluded himself that he was self-created, self-governing, who first aspired to "set himself in glory above his peers," and who, long before our first parents' rebellion, "trusted to have equall'd the most high . . . and with ambitious aim / Against the Throne and Monarchy of God / Raised impious War." For which he and his followers—one third of heaven's angels—were driven into hell, not the hell on earth described by Ulysses, but its great archetype—"bottomless perdition." In *Paradise Lost*, the story of the war in heaven becomes a cautionary tale about primal ambition told by the angel Raphael to Adam and Eve before their temptation and fall, a cautionary tale told in vain of course, and not for the last time:

> Cromwell, I charge thee, fling away ambition!
> By that sin fell the angels; how can man then
> (The image of his Maker) hope to win by it?

So the ruined Cardinal Wolsey warns his servant Thomas Cromwell in Shakespeare's (and perhaps Fletcher's) *Henry VIII*. The warning comes with the authority of bitter experience, which Cromwell has before his eyes, but the play shows us that despite all warnings, he no less urgently than Wolsey or Achilles or Eve and Adam must still be stirring in pursuit of power, wealth, and fame, insinuating himself into Henry's favor, as though to outdo his former master. "As for Cromwell," reports a courtier,

> Beside that of the Jewel House, is made Master
> O' th' Rolls, and the King's secretary; further, sir,
> Stands in the gap and trade of more preferments,
> With which the time will load him.

Shakespeare's audience would have known that the "gap and trade"—or high road—of the King's preferments would in a few years load Cromwell beyond what he could bear, and set him on the instant way to dishonor and the scaffold.

But these are high and distant animadversions drawn from ancient times and outworn ways of thinking: that the life of ambition is a kind of hell; that those who are ever stirring in pursuit of power, wealth, and fame must abandon all hope, doomed as they are to reenact the sin of Adam and Eve; that at the heart of ambition, like the serpent in the Garden, lies the desire to be a god, which God will punish. By that sin fell the angels? What? Are we to be frightened by bugbears such as these? To do so would seem almost un-American. We live in a nation that celebrates ambition and in a culture that has learned from Machiavelli and Hobbes and Locke and Adam Smith, not to mention the founders of our country, that the world would be a better place if we were to liberate our passions (some of them, at least, and prudently, of course) and especially our desire for power, fame, and wealth. From self-interest properly understood, public good will flow, guided by an invisible hand, which might be God's but which certainly is not the biblical God's, or so modern political thought promises, and the promises have proved persuasive and have transformed the world, made it richer and more powerful and even made fame, which we now call celebrity, available to people who never could have dreamed of it earlier, for which transformation Machiavelli and his followers have won immortality—or the closest thing to it that the modern world acknowledges.

In *Democracy in America*, written nearly two centuries ago but still considered one of the profoundest studies not only of the United States but of democracy generally, Alexis de Tocqueville calls attention repeatedly to the restless striving after power, fame, and wealth that characterizes life in the young United States and that marks it as a product of modern liberated currents of thought. "No Americans are devoid of a yearning desire to rise," he writes. "All are constantly seeking to acquire property, power, and reputation." "Everyone is in motion, some in quest of power, others of gain." But Tocqueville's judgment of the effects of this liberation, "this continual striving of men after fortune" is decidedly ambivalent. In a chapter titled "Why the Americans are so Restless in the midst of their Prosperity," Tocqueville compares the "tumult" of liberated and ambitious modern life to the traditional ways that can still be encountered in "certain remote corners of the Old World." There many people are ignorant and poor and backward, "yet their countenances are generally placid and their spirits light." In America, on the other hand, Tocqueville says he saw "the freest and most enlightened men placed in the happiest circumstances that the world affords," and it seemed to him that "a cloud habitually hung upon their brow, and I thought them serious and almost sad, even in their pleasures." Rather than being satisfied with what they have, they are always conscious of the race to acquire more. "It is strange to see with what feverish ardor the Americans pursue their own welfare, and to watch the vague dread that constantly torments them lest they should not have chosen the shortest path which may lead to it."

Take the instant way to feverish ardor and vague dread! Obviously Tocqueville saw that all was not well in the world's first great democracy, and that a significant part of the problem was created by the liberation of ambition. But he also believed that "the advent of democracy as a governing power in the world's affairs, universal and irresistible, was at hand," and that it would be futile to try to restore the values of the world of King James or Shakespeare or Milton. According to Tocqueville, remedies for the discontents of modern times must be consistent with modern values, which meant that the cure for the miserable pettiness of ambition that he discovered in the United States of the 1830s could not consist in seeking to repress ambition but rather in embracing it more fully. What distressed Tocqueville about ambition in America was not its ubiquity but its pettiness: "the rarity of lofty ambition to be observed in the midst of the universally ambitious stir of society."

> I confess that I apprehend much less for democratic society from
> the boldness than from the mediocrity of desires. What appears to
> me most to be dreaded is that in the midst of the small, incessant
> occupations of private life, ambition should lose its vigor and its
> greatness; the passions of man should abate, but at the same time
> be lowered; so that the march of society should every day become
> more tranquil and less aspiring.

Tocqueville's dread that "ambition should lose its vigor and its greatness" reflects his view that modern democracy stands poised between two possible futures: on the one hand, the freedom that can obtain in a nation of citizens who understand their self-interest and act upon it, and on the other, the "despotism" into which citizens may allow themselves to be lulled by a central government, powerful and paternalistic, that undertakes by itself alone "to secure their gratifications and to watch over their fate." Citizens full of vigorous ambition, Tocqueville thinks, will be immune to the charms of "soft despotism," and he goes so far as to encourage democratic leaders to "preach" the virtue of pride rather than humility.

> Thus, far from thinking that humility ought to be preached to our contemporaries, I would have endeavors made to give them a more enlarged idea of themselves and of their kind. Humility is unwholesome to them; what they most want is, in my opinion, pride. I would willingly exchange several of our small virtues for this one vice.

Brave new world of vice by which a brave new world of despotism is to be combated! Welcome, Machiavelli! Farewell, Cardinal Wolsey who found his virtue late, but at least could find it. But what kind of ambition does Tocqueville mean in practice? Surely not the ambition of a Cesare Borgia, Machiavelli's model (up to a point) in *The Prince*, whose great virtue was that he knew how and when "to enter into evil" in the pursuit of power; or of a Hannibal, whom Machiavelli praises for the "inhuman cruelty" that made it possible for him to accomplish his famous deeds? No. More prudently, Tocqueville celebrates the ambition of the first English settlers in New England, who proved themselves capable of defying despots without becoming despotic themselves. They came from relatively modest backgrounds and were the subjects of a powerful monarchy, but they set out to create something truly new, a regime radically different from the one they had left behind, a regime of equality and liberty. And led by men of genius like William Bradford at Plymouth and John Winthrop in Boston, they succeeded in making their ambition a reality. "The civilization of New England has been like a beacon lit upon a hill," writes Tocqueville, echoing Winthrop's famous phrase, "which after it has diffused its warmth immediately around it, also tinges the distant horizon."

In similarly glowing terms, Tocqueville describes the ambitious labors of "the great men whom the Revolution had created . . . George Washington [and] the finest minds and noblest characters that had ever appeared in the New World" who did not fall out with each other after their first effort to form a union (the Articles of Confederation) failed, but cooperated to form a new and enduring Constitution. It was a new thing "in the history of society to see a great people turn a calm and scrutinizing eye upon itself . . . to see it carefully examine the extent of the evil, and patiently wait two whole years until a remedy is discovered, to which it voluntarily submitted without its costing a tear or a drop of blood from mankind." Such are the benefits that may result from the operation of high ambition.

And to these examples we might add Abraham Lincoln, whose high ambition led him not to make himself a despot, which many thought he would and even should, but to thwart the hydra-headed despotism (North and South) that threatened what the early settlers and the great men of the Revolution had accomplished. Which great task Lincoln did not accomplish without political maneuvers that Machiavelli would have viewed with admiration.

But what is that clanking in the attic? The sound of rusty mail now out of fashion? Mere bugbears in the gap and trade of more preferments?

✧

I grew up in a mill town in Maine during and just after the Second World War, a thriving but unglamorous place, nothing at all like the picturesque villages along the coast where artists and millionaires mingled with lobster men, and even less like the wild expanse of forest and lakes to the west and north, the domain of sports and their guides, loggers and logger barons. Along the handsome and polluted river that drove the mills and carried their wastes down to the distant ocean stretched the tenements where the mill workers, mostly French-Canadian and Irish, lived; the businesses that served them and all of us, purveying just about everything the body could require, including some things that my mother thought ought not to be purveyed; the banks, an amazing number by today's standards, all small, strictly local, and each fiercely ambitious to outdo the others, many standing on quite doubtful financial foundations (as likely as any ice cream parlor to liquidate tomorrow, said my father); an equally amazing number of churches of various and conflicting doctrines—Saint Pat's and Saint Joe's and Saint Peter's (all three Roman Catholic, of course, but the first two Irish and the last French, and inclined to consider themselves as belonging to two quite different religions), the Congregationalists, the Universalists, the Baptists, the Methodists, the Episcopalians, and others, even a small synagogue; two hospitals, one run by nuns, the other by Protestant businessmen. Needless to say, the churches and the hospitals were just as ambitious to best each other as the banks and the businesses were. Cooperation among rivals was rare, Saint Pat's suspicions about the goings on at Saint Peter's being just as dark as the Baptists' suspicions about the Universalists. And vice versa. The annual French-Irish baseball game, representing as it did a contest between competing gods, or at least patron saints, was an event to which my mother would not let me go, even though one of my cousins, who was not French or Irish or Catholic but rather a well-known Protestant semipro with a wicked fast ball and a big stick, sometimes made a late-innings appearance on the mound for the Irish. Which appearance was likely to precipitate an awful brawl.

A few blocks back from the river, which as spring wore on grew increasingly malodorous, stood the brick and stone buildings of an academically respectable and very sobersided little college of Baptist origin, and around the college spread the pleasant but quite modest neighborhood in which my family lived among the families of professors. My father worked in one of the small banks, where he had begun during the depression as an unpaid messenger and where he eventually rose to become president. My mother, the daughter of a farmer from a nearby town where farming still flourished in its modest hardscrabble, backcountry Maine fashion, ran the house and tended to the upbringing of my brother, sister, and me, not requiring in that department the assistance of my father except on those occasions that necessitated the application of his razor strop to my or my brother's bottom. Three blows only—a rare but invariably, as I remember it, just chastisement.

My father and mother were good and loving parents, good citizens, good people, and churchgoers, though I doubt they had reflected much on the second and third chapters of Genesis or on the fact that the roots of the modern world, including the history of the United States, can be traced back to Machiavelli. Ambition was a character trait for which they had just about the highest regard, and they often urged me and my brother (my sister less, which no doubt reflected their old-fashioned view of girls) to aim as high as we could for power, wealth, and fame. Indeed, I remember that it was a common disparagement of certain of my friends deemed to be potentially bad influences on me that they "had no ambition." On the other hand, my father's career, rising from unpaid messenger to head cashier and then vice president while I was still a boy at home, was an example of ambition to be emulated, and so was the life of his father, who had left school after the sixth grade to help support his widowed mother and his younger brothers, and ended up a modestly wealthy man by our standards in that unglamorous part of Maine. His acts of generosity—helping neighbors during hard times, helping worthy boys and girls get an education, and so on—were well-known local versions of the philanthropy of other ambitious men who had become truly rich and truly famous. For example, the man who, though he had never lived among us, had made a fortune from our most successful mill and used some of his gains to endow our little college, which, as a result, had changed its name to his. Or the famous Andrew Carnegie, whose gift had created our library, a handsome granite structure that stood out among the banks and women's shops and haberdasheries and mills because of its dedication to higher things.

Through my parents and grandparents I knew how the fruits of ambition might contribute to the common good, and even tasted those fruits, reading in our library's hushed walnut-paneled rooms, attending plays and concerts at our college, exploring the leafy precincts of its campus, learning to ski on the little "mountain" half a mile from my home that the college could afford to protect from development. Even then, I believe, I had some sense of the argument that the liberation of ambition could be beneficial in ways that ambition itself, perhaps, did not envisage. However, it was hard experience rather than soft pleasure that convinced me that my parents were right to stress the importance of ambition; it was obvious that the competitive urge to get ahead at least in power and reputation was essential to the life boys lived in my hometown. Ambition was in the air we breathed. To escape it, one would have had to stop breathing.

On the school playground, along the streets of every neighborhood from the river to the college, in the driveways or backyards of houses where we congregated, in the empty lots we turned into football or baseball fields, rough and tumble competition prevailed, and could not—at least not without shame—be avoided. One had to aim to be first or risk being nothing. Although there were no gangs in those days, no Myrmidons and no real violence, at least not in my town, the world of boys was nonetheless a fair simulacrum of the world of Achilles and Hector at a lower level of mayhem. A fight was always imminent, waiting only for a taunt or a queer look to break out into blows, head locks, twisted arms, invitations to say "uncle," obscene retorts, and at the end when it was time to go home to supper, insults in the waning light, and possibly a final snowball or rock launched at the back of a retreating rival who was also a friend. Not to turn one's back on a rival until you were out of range was a rule we learned early and an adage that must be enshrined somewhere in *The Prince*.

Money was not involved in this unending competition to establish oneself, even if only for ten minutes, at the top. Reputation and power were the objects of the game, and I played it along with the rest, even with some enthusiasm, for I adopted the ambition of the world I lived in, and even

49

had some success, although not without many a humiliation, especially in fist fights, for I lacked the quick hands and willingness to take a punch in order to land one with which some of my rivals and friends were blessed. On Sundays in the United Baptist Church, sitting beside my parents and my siblings and surrounded by the mild and pacific congregation of professors and their wives, I often asked God, speaking only to Him, to give me a stronger jab, a quicker hook, and make me less shy of being smacked in the nose. Unfortunately, I never could discern that God answered this prayer except possibly once, which I will come to. If I had thought to ask Him to make me a god, I believe I would have.

One of the great strengths of the United Baptist Church in our unglamorous mill town was that Sunday School was devoted to studying the Bible. The Bible and maybe a rousing rendition of "Onward Christian Soldiers" or "A Mighty Fortress Is Our God": that was it. No ambitious schemes to alert us to world poverty; we had plenty of poverty in the tenements of our own town and from time to time the United Baptist Church, including us young people, tried to do something about it, but not in Sunday School. No lessons designed to wheedle us into talking about problems we might have observed in our homes. Nothing intended to persuade us to have more self-esteem. No. Just the Bible read aloud very earnestly and clearly by one of the splendid cohort of faculty wives who served as our teachers, followed by a bit of commentary and discussion, including recitations by us from memory. That was where I first studied with intense interest and a salutary dose of fear the story of the creation and the fall, and where I first encountered the notion that the original sin of Eve and Adam was the ambition to be a god, though my teacher did not put it quite that way; she said that when Adam and Eve disobeyed God's one commandment, they showed that they held themselves "above" or "before" God, superior to Him, which was as deep a sin as one could commit. And we could all understand this, she claimed, looking very serious, if we reflected that we did exactly the same thing, violating God's commandments, practically every day, when we told a lie, even a small one, or when we stole or coveted something our neighbor had or when we did not keep the Sabbath holy. When we did such things or failed to do other things, she said, we effectively put ourselves above God by demonstrating that we held our own judgment to be superior to His. Which struck me like a thunderbolt, for I had done such things, just as she said I had, although I did not yet understand them as manifestations of ambition. In fact, it took writing this essay to make me remember and see that connection, and also to make me meditate on the story that concludes this essay, which is the following.

There was one part of my hometown (besides the baseball field on the day of the French-Irish baseball game) where I was expressly forbidden to go. That was the stretch of uninhabited woods and brush between the river and the railroad tracks upstream from a vast cemetery where the town roads dwindled rapidly to paths and disappeared. "Up the tracks" the place was called, for the tracks were said to be the only way in and out, and people said you didn't want to go in because you weren't likely to get out. During the Great Depression, which was officially over, having been vanquished at last by the War, "up the tracks" had become a hangout for bums, wandering, more or less lawless men, men without ambition, the opposite of what men should be, who kept body and soul together only God and they knew how, and who were considered a plague upon decent people. Some were said to be still there, preferring their outlaw life to the work that was now available in the mills and the shipyards, not to mention the army. My mother said murders had been committed on innocent citizens, including boys, "up the tracks," and although my father claimed that was nonsense, he agreed that "up the tracks" was a bad place and made me promise never to go there. Naturally I wanted very much to go.

As did most of my friends, with the result that boasting of one's intention to do so became a regular part of our strident, chafing lives, including a fight or two between boasters who mocked each other's boasts until one day a boy announced that he had done what everyone else was talking about and done it alone. Pushed to "prove it," he added details, a lot of them—how he had found a bum sitting on the tracks, who had showed him a pearl-handled revolver but had not shot anything; how the bum had given him a cigarette, which he had smoked while the bum smoked too and told him stories about California where you could live by picking fruit from trees that grew right along the railroad tracks. On the way back, the boy said, he had found four dollars and fifty cents lying on the ties between the rails. The money was now in a metal box at home, where he had promised his father to leave it. This story, which came out slowly and not without some hesitations, false starts, and even contradictions, was received with considerable skepticism, especially the parts about the cigarette and the money, but most of us, I think, were tormented by the suspicion that our friend might really have done what he claimed to have done. And done it without us.

For a long time I lay sleepless that night, going over what I had heard and working up a plan to go "up the tracks" myself as soon as I could get away unnoticed. Sunday after dinner when my parents would be visiting with my grandparents or maybe even taking a nap, would be a good time, I thought. I could sneak away when the meal was over and get back before supper, which was informal and late on the Sabbath. Just before falling asleep I determined to undertake this adventure alone, but in the morning I decided to ask a friend to go along, who took some persuading. It turned out he too had promised his parents not to go "up the tracks," and he did not think he should break his promise without a good reason. Which I was ready for, having been looking for reasons myself. "First of all," I told him, "your parents will never know." He frowned and looked thoughtful. "Second of all," I went on, "there's no real danger. From what I hear from my father all the talk about murders is nonsense. There haven't been any." He nodded but continued frowning. "And third of all, we're not babies any more. We're in grammar school, and we've got to grow up sometime." I could see this impressed him. "And finally of all, I want to be the first one to go 'up the tracks' and see it for myself." He looked puzzled and said we couldn't be the first because our friend had been there. To which I replied I did not believe he had, and that in any case he couldn't prove it, which we would be able to. "You can vouch for me and I can vouch for you," I said. "He's got nobody to vouch for him but the bums. We'll be the first. You aren't afraid, are you?"

That Sunday after dinner I found him sitting on the lush grass among the tombstones in his family plot. He seemed to be watching, but apparently he didn't spot me coming because he jumped when I spoke. "My father asked where I was going," I said. "I told him I was going to find out what you were doing. Which was true." "No it wasn't," he said. "You already knew." He sounded as though he wanted to pick a fight, which was tempting but I held my peace. The tracks, when we found them at the top of a steep slope of loose gravel and cinders, surprised us. The area into which they led was desolate and barren, the trees stunted and the bushes covered with leathery leaves, but the rails themselves shone, scoured by the great wheels of the trains whose whistles we could hear in our beds at night, headed we knew not where. We discussed what to do if a train should appear. My friend had heard that one should get quite a ways off the track. "How far?" I asked. He didn't know, but far—very far or one might be struck by a moving part. At which I laughed. Trains were more dangerous than people thought, he said firmly as though he were speaking to a child. He had also heard that if you put a penny on a rail for a train to run over and flatten it, which some people did just for fun, the penny could derail the train. I had heard that too, but it didn't seem likely, and I said so, at which he laughed.

It was just then that we saw the bum. He was crouched between the rails like a runner on a track waiting for the starting gun. "There he is," I said in a whisper just as though I knew who he was and had expected to see him. "He's no bigger than we are," my friend whispered. For a long moment we both stood unmoving, staring at the bum as though he were a strange bird or beast, but he must have become conscious of us somehow because he turned and saw us and, still crouching, sprang down the bank, disappearing into the brush at the bottom. When he reappeared among the leaves, he was heading for the river.

My friend grabbed my arm to hold me, but I pulled away and skidded down the bank into the brush too, thinking I would go alone if I had to, but he followed, and we thrashed across the rough ground one after the other, trading the lead as one of us found the easier way and then the other, little by little gaining on our man. When we came out of the brush onto a ledge above the river, the bum turned, panting, and faced us, and I saw with a shock that he was very old, older than my grandfather, and that his face and head were as hairless as a reptile's.

"What do you want with me?" he asked. Twenty feet below the ledge the yellow river swirled and hissed. "We wanted to catch you," said my friend before I could think of an answer. "Catch me?" said the bum. "You guys must want to be in the papers." His eyes closed and opened. One hand went into a pocket and when it came out it was holding a knife, the kind that has a blade you can switch in and out by pushing a button. "Now get out of here," he said, "and don't come back if you can help it." My friend went, but I didn't dare turn my back. "Go on," said the bum. "Your friend's smarter than you are." I took a couple of steps backward, still watching the knife. Suddenly it clicked and the blade snapped out. "Get," said the bum, and I went too, running for my life, hunching my back against the blow that never came.

In the cemetery, my friend was waiting. Sitting on the broad plot that still had plenty of room for him and his family, we recovered our nerve, discussing what we had done and what we had escaped, wondering whether the bum had meant to kill us or not, and pretty soon we began to disagree about this and that, and started to get angry. "That was a dumb thing to do," my friend said. "Yes," I said, though not very comfortably because he made his comment sound like an accusation of me. "And a bad thing," he went on. "I never would have done it if it hadn't been for you." Which led to an escalating quarrel and finally to one of the hardest fist fights I have ever been in. At first it seemed to me that God was at last rewarding me by giving me the stiffer jab and quicker hook that I had been asking Him to give me for quite a while. But my friend was really the better fighter and at the end, though we were both pretty bloody, I was the one who said "uncle." At home I found my father dozing in his study. He woke up fast, however, when he saw me, and asked for the facts, which I gave him, including everything beginning with the lie I had told when I left after dinner. At the end of my confession, I suggested that perhaps I had paid for my sins already in having been terrified by the bum and beaten up by my friend, but my father would have none of that. If I had thought of it, I might have asked him for clemency on the ground that I had at least shown significant signs of ambition, but perhaps it was just as well I didn't think of it. My father went for his razor strop and administered the usual three sharp strokes, which I richly deserved.

5

Ambition

Lilies That Fester

Eugene H. Peterson

THE ONE PIECE OF mail certain to go into my wastebasket unread is the letter addressed to the "busy pastor." Not that the phrase doesn't describe me at times, but I refuse to give my attention to someone who encourages what is worst in me.

Before becoming a pastor I had always understood myself as ambitious. I wanted to do well academically and in athletics, and I did. I wanted to do my best with what I had been given. I wanted to please my parents, my teachers, my coaches. And for the most part I did.

At the age of twenty-four I was ordained by the Presbyterian Church (USA) to be a pastor. I was still ambitious—it was wired into my genes—but my ambition now expanded to include a sense of responsibility to a way of life, a vocation, that included a lot more than just being true to myself. In my ordination I took vows to preserve a theological tradition, be "in subjection to [my] brethren in the Lord," take responsibility for leading men and women in the way of Jesus and caring for their souls. I found it exhilarating. I had never been more "myself." But at the same time I found that there was far more to me than myself; I was "not my own."

I assumed that my life as a Christian believer would quite naturally evolve and develop into being a Christian pastor. I supposed that the path of personal faith in Jesus that I had been traveling since childhood now with ordination had widened into an Isaianic highway in the American wilderness. Who I was as a Christian extended vocationally into living as a pastor. My work would converge with my baptismal identity: my work an extension of my faith, vocation serving as paving to make the faith accessible for others who wished to travel this road.

It didn't turn out that way. The French have a wonderful phrase, *deformation professionelle*, that pinpointed what I was experiencing—a liability, a tendency to defect that is inherent in the role one has assumed as, say, a physician, a lawyer, a pastor, or priest. The physician is deformed into a doctor dealing with "cases" and "illnesses" but not persons with names and stories. Or the lawyer becomes more concerned in winning a case for his client than caring for justice. If there is a deformation to which I as a pastor was subject, it was becoming a shopkeeper in religious goods and services. A lot of people expected me to help them or serve them in ways that had nothing to do with what God had called me to do. And, of course, being a person who wants to please people (pastors are particularly vulnerable here), I was in danger of doing my best to please people on their terms, not in the terms to which I had taken vows to fulfill. I wasn't taking the time to be present, to listen; personal relationships became thin. I found myself depersonalizing men and women and youth into "problems" to be fixed or "resources" to be exploited. As demands on my time increased, I was becoming a very busy shopkeeper. Without my noticing, the ambition to do my best to keep the vows of my ordination, giving witness to salvation and caring for the souls of my congregation, was being eroded to an impersonal role of making people feel better about themselves.

When I came across the term *deformation professionelle*, it became a diagnostic tool that exposed my pastoral busyness defined by Hilary of Tours as *irreligiosa sollicitudo pro Deo*, "a blasphemous anxiety to do God's work for him."* Hilary got my attention: ambition deformed into mere busyness.

On reflection I realized that I had become busy, a bastard form of ambition, for two reasons.

I am busy because I am vain. I want to appear important. Significant. What better way than to be busy? The incredible hours, the crowded schedule, the heavy demands on my time are proof to myself—and to all who will notice—that I am important. If I go into a doctor's office and find there

---

* I learned *irreligiosa sollicitudo pro Deo* from my spiritual director, a Carmelite nun, as she did her best to accustom me to a contemplative life. Her Latin phrase has stuck in my memory ever since.

is no one waiting and see through a half-open door the doctor reading a book, I wonder if he's any good. A good doctor will have people lined up waiting to see him; a good doctor will not have time to read a book. Although I grumble about waiting my turn in a busy doctor's office, I am impressed with his importance.

Such experiences affect me. I live in a society in which crowded schedules and harassed conditions are evidence of importance, so I develop a crowded schedule and harassed conditions. When others notice, they acknowledge my significance, and my vanity is fed.

I am busy because I am lazy. I indolently let others decide what I will do instead of resolutely deciding myself. I let people who do not understand the work of the pastor write the agenda for my day's work because I am too slipshod to write it myself. The pastor is a shadow figure in most people's minds, a marginal person vaguely connected with matters of God and good will. Anything remotely religious or somehow well-intentioned can be properly assigned to the pastor.

Because these assignments to pastoral service are made sincerely, I go along with them. It takes effort to refuse, and besides, there's always the danger that the refusal will be interpreted as a rebuff, a betrayal of religion, and a calloused disregard for people in need.

It was a favorite theme of C. S. Lewis that only lazy people work hard. By lazily abdicating the essential work of deciding and directing, establishing values and setting goals, other people do it for us; and then we find ourselves frantically, at the last minute, trying to satisfy a half dozen different demands on our time, none of which is essential to our vocation, to stave off the disaster of disappointing someone.

But if I vainly crowd my day with conspicuous activity or let others fill my day with imperious demands, I don't have time to do my proper work, the work to which I have been called. How can I lead people into the quiet place beside the still waters if I am in perpetual motion? How can I persuade a person to live by faith and not by works if I have to juggle my schedule constantly to make everything fit into place?

Now that I had a name for it, I realized I was not the only one. It seemed pretty widespread in the American church as "pastor" and "church" were relentlessly being functionalized by an obsession with statistics in place of the cure of souls and a vigorous implementation of depersonalized programs that essentially displaced the cultivation of reverent and worshipful attentiveness in the relationship with God.

It would never have occurred to me that ambition, which had served me so well for so long, could go so wrong. I later remembered Shakespeare's wonderful phrase, "Lilies that fester smell far worse than weeds." Which is to say, the worst is the corruption of the best.

⊖

Like Dives in hell, I was genuinely astonished. I had presumed that the life I had been living personally would naturally issue vocationally into something blessed. Here I was experiencing instead "a great chasm" between my personal faith and my professional work. Like Dives in hell I began praying "have mercy upon me, and send Lazarus to dip the tip of his finger in water and cool my tongue" (Luke 16:26, 24 NRSV).

I began looking around for help. Lazarus never showed up, but with some help from friends I began to uncover writers who gave me the needed perspective and insight. It came as something of a surprise to find that the allies most useful in keeping my work a true vocation and not devolving into a religious job were not the theologians and scholars who had been my teachers but creative artists who wrote novels and poems. And I soon recognized the reason. Creation, the Spirit hovering over the waters, descending like a dove on Jesus, is the very breath of life, whether in church or workplace or home.

I wake up in the middle of this creative work every morning. But the Spirit work of creation takes place mostly behind the scenes and is invisible for the most part. The most visible parts of my work—preaching sermons and administering programs—can be done with apparent competence quite apart from anything relational, prayerful, or compassionate.

Most of the books given to me by my teachers were intended to help me in these visible areas. But what I was praying for was help in the invisible parts—the creative center. Creation and re-creation—living to the glory of God—is the core of the gospel, the Spirit's work. But when this Spirit-Creation center gets moved to the periphery, "creative" means nothing more than "interesting" or "innovative." Who is there to keep me aware of the very nature of creation, the work that goes into it, the way it feels?

I knew I needed to find a way to keep ambition from deforming my vocation into something that I felt in my bones was squeezing the Spirit out of my life, professionalizing and depersonalizing my life into a role in which I was too busy to take time with the complexities of people or be present before God. I found it by happening on writers who I am sure didn't have a pastor in mind when they wrote their books, but for me they were Lazarus dipping his finger into water. Over the years I found many. Here are three of the early ones who cooled my busy, overheated tongue: James Joyce, Wallace Stegner, and Wendell Berry.

∽

James Joyce

The first book on pastoral work that meant anything to me either personally or vocationally was Joyce's novel *Ulysses*. Two-thirds of the way into this meander of narrative, I saw what I could be doing, should be doing, as a pastor. Previous to *Ulysses*, I had never looked on the workaday aspects of my work as particularly creative. I knew they were important, and I accepted them as necessary tasks to be carried out whether I felt like it or not, but except for occasional epiphanies I did not find them very interesting. Nearly everything else I did, the public aspects where I had an audience, pulled the best out of me, pushed me to my limits. Calling on the lonely, visiting the sick, sitting with the dying, making small talk before a meeting were more or less routine functions that could be accomplished satisfactorily with a modest investment of tact, compassion, and faithfulness. Just showing up was the main thing.

And then one day while reading *Ulysses*, at about page 611, an earthquake opened a fissure at my feet and all my assumptions of ordinariness dropped into it. All those routines of the pastoral vocation suddenly were no longer "routines."

Leopold Bloom, the Ulysses of Joyce's story is a very ordinary man. No detail in his life is distinguished, unless it might be his monotone ordinariness. And Dublin, the city in which he lives, is a very ordinary city with nothing to distinguish it other than its depressing ordinariness.

This colorless, undistinguished human being in this colorless undistinguished place provides the content for the novel. James Joyce narrates a single day in the life of the Dublin Jew, Leopold Bloom. Detail by detail Joyce takes us though a day in the life of this person, a day in which nothing of note happens. But as the details accumulate, observed with such acute and imaginative (pastoral!) care, the realization begins to develop that, common as they are, these details are all uniquely human. Flickers of recognition signal memories of the old myth; Homer's grand telling of the adventure of the Greek Ulysses as he traveled all the country of experience and possibility and found himself finally home.

Joyce woke me up to the infinity of meaning within the limitations of the ordinary person in the ordinary day. Leopold Bloom buying and sell-ing, talking and listening, eating and defecating, praying and blaspheming is mythic in the grand manner. The twenty-year-long voyage from Troy to Ithaca is repeated every twenty-four hours in anyone's life if we only have eyes and ears for it. Now I knew my work: this is the pastor's work, grounded in the ordinary. I wanted to be able to look at each person in my parish with the same imagination and insight and comprehensiveness with which Joyce looked at Leopold Bloom, whether anyone noticed or not. The story line is different. The story being worked out right before my eyes, if only I can stay awake long enough to see it, is not the Greek story of Ulysses but the gospel story of Jesus. The means are different—Joyce was a writer using a pencil and I am a pastor practicing prayer—but we are doing the same thing, seeing the marvelous interlacings of history and sexuality and religion and culture and place in this person, on this day.

I saw now that I had two sets of story to get straight. I already knew the gospel story pretty well. I was a preacher, after all, a proclaimer with a message. I had learned the original languages of the story, been immersed by my education in its long development and taught how to translate it into the present. I was steeped in the theology that kept my mind safe and hon-est in the story, conversant in the history that gave perspective and propor-tion. In the pulpit and behind the lectern I read and told this story. I love doing this, love reading and pondering and preaching these Gospel stories, making them accessible to people in a different culture, with different expe-riences, living in different weather, under different politics. It is privileged and glorious work. This was work I expected to do when I became a pastor, and it was work for which I was adequately trained.

But this other set of stories, the stories being lived in my congrega-tion—the stories of Mary Vaughn and Jack Tyndale, Nancy Lion and Bruce MacIntosh, Abigail Davidson and Olaf Odegaard—I had to get these sto-ries straight too. The Jesus story was being reworked and re-experienced in each of these people, in this town, this day. And I was here to see them take shape, listen to sentences being formed, observe actions, discern character and plot. I determined to be as exegetically serious when listening to Eric Matthews in *koine* American as I was when reading St. Matthew in *koine*

Greek. I wanted to see the Jesus story in the stories of each person in my congregation with as much local detail and raw experience as James Joyce did with the Ulysses story in the person of Leopold Bloom and his Dublin friends and neighbors.

The Jesuit poet Gerard Manley Hopkins gave me a text for my work:

> For Christ plays in ten thousand places,
> Lovely in limbs, and lovely in eyes not his
> To the Father through the features of men's faces.

From that moment until now, visits to home and hospital, calls on the lonely, sitting with the dying, listening in on conversations, and providing spiritual direction have been the primary occasions for getting time for this work, access to these stories. A lot more than tact and compassion and faithfulness are required now. There is a lot more to this than "showing up." I find myself listening for nuances, making connections, remembering and anticipating, watching how the verbs work ("that's an aorist; is this a subjunctive?"), watching for signs of atonement, reconciliation, sanctification, I am sitting before these people as Joyce sat before his writing desk, watching for the invisible to emerge into visibility, the silence to take on flesh, watching and listening for rushing wind and tongues of the Spirit's fire.

Confinement by illness or weakness or appointment to a single room from which most of the traffic of the world is excluded and to which most of the fashion of the world is indifferent provides limits that encourage concentration and observation. Deprived of distracting stimuli, I found that attentiveness increases. Cut off the numerous possibilities and choices that are usual for me, I find that I am capable of attending to the actuality of the present. This life, just as it is; not what is coming next, but what is going on now. Sitting with the dying is an exercise in "now-ness." The bare simplicity of life itself is there for wonder and appreciation; sitting with the living provides the same exercise if I embrace it as such.

Over the course of years, most of the families in a pastor's congregation encounter illness or confinement or death of one kind or another. Since my Joycean conversion I no longer consider my visits at these times as the duties of pastoral care but as occasions for original research on the stories being shaped in lives by the living Christ. I go to these appointments with the same diligence and curiosity that I bring to a page of Isaiah's oracles or a tangled argument in St. Paul.

There is a text for this work in St. Mark's Gospel: "He has risen . . . he is going before you to Galilee; there you will see him, as he told you" (16:6–7 RSV). In every visit, every meeting I attend, every appointment I keep, I have been anticipated. The risen Christ got there ahead of me. The risen Christ is in that room already. What is he doing? What is he saying? What is going on?

In order to fix the implications of that text in my vocation, I have taken to quoting it before every visit or meeting: "He is risen . . . he is going before you to 1020 Emmorton Road; there you will see him as he told you." Later in the day it will be: "He is risen . . . he is going before you to St. Joseph's Hospital; there you will see him, as he told you." When I arrive and enter the room, I am not so much wondering what I am going to do or say that will be pastoral as I am alert and observant for what the risen Christ has been doing that is making a gospel story out of this life. The theological category for this is "prevenience," the priority of grace.

Ambition grounded in the ordinary prevents it from being squandered in busyness.

⊸

Wallace Stegner

Life has a story shape. The most adequate rendering of the world is through storytelling. It is the least specialized and most comprehensive form of language. Everything and anything can be put into the story. And the moment it is in the story it develops meaning, participates in plot, becomes somehow or other significant. The entire biblical revelation comes to us in the form of story. Nothing less than story is adequate to the largeness and intricacy of the truth of creation and redemption.

The verbal effects of sin result in the obfuscation of story, the fragmentation of story into disconnected anecdotes, the reduction of story to gossip, the dismemberment of story into lists or formulae or rules. Most of the words that come before us each day are delivered by television, newspaper, and magazine journalists. There is no story in them beyond the immediate event, the speech, the accident. There is nothing that connects to the past, reaches into the future, or soars to the heights. Instead of connecting with more reality, the words disconnect us, leaving us in a boneyard of incident and comment.

Every time someone tells a story and tells it well and truly, the gospel is served. Out of the chaos of incident and accident, story-making words bring light, coherence and connecting, meaning and value. If there is a story, then maybe, just maybe, there is (must be!) a Storyteller.

Wallace Stegner served me as one of the premier storytellers in my life. I grew up in the West in a kind of anarchist/populist atmosphere. We sat loose to authority and had no sense of continuity with the past. The town I grew up in was only forty years old when I arrived in it. I had no sense of tradition. The Scandinavia of my grandparents was half a world away, and the Kootenai and Salish Indians who were native to the valley I grew up in were not ancestors in any living sense.

People moved around a lot, looking for a "better deal." We moved ten times during my growing up. Experiences were intense and sometimes glorious, but they were not part of anything large or historic, and my understanding of the gospel was thereby reduced to the temporary and the "better deal."

In his early novel *The Big Rock Candy Mountain*, Stegner wrote a story using the materials of my life. He grew up a couple of hundred miles from me (but thirty years earlier) in a town not unlike mine. As I read his novel about the American/Canadian West and its people, I recognize in it most of the people I grew up with, and also the feelings I had, the language I learned and used, the wanderlust and loneliness, the rootless and religionless poverty/prosperity. As an adult, I was in danger of rejecting all of that in favor of something more congenial to what I fantasized as a Christian culture with all problems solved and all prayers answered. Stegner's storytelling put the materials of my actual experience—the land and weather, the slang and customs, the bullies and the bloody noses, the jerry-built towns and makeshift jobs—into a story. He made a cosmos out of it, showed this country and people as capable of plot and coherence as anything in Homer's Greece or St. Mark's Galilee.

I now find it significant that it was not the pastor in my congregation or professor in my seminary who did this for me, but a novelist who trained my imagination to take in everything around me with the realization that I am worth the attention of an Author. By now my library of scholars and theologians who help me understand the Bible and Christian faith has expanded to include a growing company of novelists who help me understand the men and women in my congregation as participants in something large and purposeful—the story of creation and salvation. None of the people I grew up with thought of themselves that way, worthy of the attention of an author. We were neither interesting enough nor important enough to be included in a plot.

It was a turning point for me. No longer would I take a journalist's view of anyone—good for an hour or so of attention but only if they happen into an accident or win a prize.

The persons to whom this gospel story is proclaimed are, each of them, one-of-kind. Baron Friedrich von Hugel was fond of saying, "There are no dittos among souls." At school I learned to marvel that no two snowflakes are the same, no two oak leaves identical. From snowflakes and leaves I gradually moved on to grasp the intensification of the unique that takes place in the human being. As much as I have in common with the other parts of creation, when it comes to being human there is nothing quite like me. And as much as I have in common with all other humans, when it comes to being me, I am far more different from everyone I meet than alike. A true hearing of the gospel always takes in the specifically personal. "I have called you by name" has become an essential element in my pastoral vocation (Isa 43:1 RSV).

Meanwhile, world conditions are constantly at work eroding the high profile specifics of named persons by giving them labels: Extomorph, Unsaved, Anorexic, Bipolar, Single Parent, Diabetic, Tither, Left-brained. The labels are marginally useful for understanding some aspect or other of the human condition, but the moment they are used to identify a person, they obscure the very thing that I am most interested in; the unprecedented, unrepeatable soul addressed by God.

Every time someone is addressed by name and realizes that in the meeting they are being treated as one-of-a-kind—not as a customer, not as a patient, not as a voter, not as a Presbyterian, not as a sinner—the gospel is served. Saving love is always personally specific, never merely generic. Christ's mercy is always customized to a discrete history, never swallowed up in abstraction. A good novelist provides me with eyes to see past the labels, ears to hear beneath stereotyping clichés.

Ambition grounded in story prevents the reduction of souls to cartoon caricatures.

✐

Wendell Berry

Wendell is a farmer in Kentucky. On this farm, besides plowing fields, planting crops, and working horses, he writes novels and poems and essays. The importance of place is a recurrent theme—place embraced and loved, understood and honored. Whenever Berry writes the word "farm," I substitute "parish." The sentence works for me every time.

Berry convinced me that it is absurd to resent my place: my place is that without which I cannot do my work. Parish work is every bit as physical as farm work: it is these people, under these conditions, in this place. So it is not my task to impose a different way of life on these people in this place but to work with what is already here. There is a kind of modern farmer, Berry tells me, who is impatient with the actual conditions of any farm and brings in big equipment to eliminate what is distinctively local so that machines can do their work unimpeded by local quirks and idiosyncrasies. They treat the land not as a resource to be cared for but as loot to be plundered.

When I see my congregation as raw material to manufacture into an evangelism program or a mission outreach or a learning center, before I know it I'm pushing and pulling, cajoling and seducing, persuading and selling. It would not be nearly as bad if my congregation resisted and resented and challenged when I work out of this attitude, but they are so used to being treated this way by businesses, public relation firms, educators, medical practitioners, and politicians that they don't see anything amiss when I also do it. (And, in fact, when I don't do it, or quit doing it, they wonder why I'm not acting like a "pastor" anymore.)

It is a highly effective way to develop a religious organization. People are motivated to do fine things, join meaningful programs, contribute to wonderful causes. The returns in numbers and applause are considerable. But in the process I find myself dealing more and more in causes and generalities and abstractions, judging success by numbers, giving less and less attention to particular people, and experiencing a rapidly blurred memory of the complex interactions of crisscrossed histories that are my workplace.

Berry is unyielding and prescient in these matters. "The Devil's work is abstraction"—not the love of material things but the love of their quantities—which, of course, is why "David's heart smote him after he had numbered the people" (2 Sam 24:10 RSV). It is not the lover of material things but the abstractionist who defends long-term damage for short-term gain, or who calculates the "acceptability" of industrial damage to ecological or human health, or who counts dead bodies on the battlefield. "The true lover of material things does not think in this way, but is answerable instead to the paradox of the parable of the lost sheep: that each is more precious than all."

Religious work-in-general is not pastoral work—it interferes with it. It makes a muddle of the gospel. Berry has convinced me from his life on the farm that my work is not to make a religious establishment succeed but to nurture the gospel of Jesus Christ into maturity. Holiness cannot be imposed; it must grow from the inside. I never know how Christ is going to appear in another person, let alone in a congregation. I must be mindful of the conditions, treating as ever more particular and precious each of these parishioners.

When I work with particulars, I develop a reverence for what is actually there instead of contempt for what is not, inadequacies that seduce me into a covetousness for someplace else. A farm, Berry contends, is a kind of small-scale ecosystem, everything working with everything else in certain rhythms and proportions. The farmer's task is to understand the rhythms and the proportions and then to nurture their health, not bullying, not invading the place and deciding that it is going to function on his rhythms and according to the size of his ego. If all a farmer is after is profit, he will not be reverential before what is actually there but only greedy for what he can get out of it.

The parallel with my parish could not be more exact. I substitute my pastoral vocabulary for Berry's agricultural and find Berry urging me to be mindful of my congregation, in reverence before it. These are souls, divinely worked on souls, whom the Spirit is shaping for eternal habitations. Long before I arrive on the scene, the Spirit is at work. I must fit into what is going on. I have no idea yet what is taking place here; I must study the contours, understand the weather, know what kind of crops grow in this climate, be in awe before the complex intricacies between past and present, between the people in the parish and those outside.

And topsoil. Berry has taught me a lot about topsoil. I had never paid attention to it before. I was amazed to find that the dirt under my feet, which I treat like dirt, is a treasure—millions of organisms constantly interacting, a constant cycle of death and resurrection, the source of most of the world's food. There are a few people who respect and nourish and protect the topsoil. There are many others who rapaciously strip-mine it. Still others are merely careless, and out of ignorance expose it to wind and water erosion. Right now as I write this in my study, I can hear large earthmovers across the road rearranging the contours of eight acres of farmland in preparation for building a school. The topsoil is in the way and so is scraped off, leaving firmer clay for a base. The topsoil will be replaced by cement and asphalt. This is going on all the time, all over America. Topsoil is disappearing at an alarming rate.

Berry says, "In talking about topsoil, it is hard to avoid the language of religion." Congregation is the topsoil in pastoral work. This is the material substance in which all the Spirit's work takes place—these people, assembled in worship, dispersed in blessing. They are so ordinary, so unobtrusively there. It is easy to take them for granted, quit seeing the interactive energies. I become preoccupied in building my theological roads, mission constructs, and parking-lot curricula, that is, start treating this precious congregational topsoil as something dead and inert to be rearranged to suit my vision, and then bulldoze whatever isn't immediately useful to the sidelines where it won't interfere with my projects.

But this is the field of my work, just as it is, teeming with energy, nutrients, mixing death and life. I cannot manufacture it but I can protect it. I can nourish it. I can refrain from polluting or violating it. But mostly, like the farmer with his topsoil, I must respect and honor and reverence it, be in awe before the vast mysteries contained in its unassuming ordinariness.

The congregation is topsoil—seething with energy and organisms that have incredible capacities for assimilating death and participating in resurrection. The only biblical stance is awe, fear of the Lord. When I see what is before me, really before me, I take off my shoes before the burning bush of congregation.

If I am dismissive of the uniqueness of this parish, or unwilling to acknowledge it, I will impose my routines on it for a few seasons, harvest a few souls, then move on to another parish to try my luck there, and in my belligerent folly miss the beauty and holiness and sheer Divine life that was there all the time, unseen and unheard because of my rapacious ambition.

James Freeman Clarke, an Easterner who traveled in the West in the nineteenth century, wrote in his book *Self-Culture*, that at one time a phrenologist came to his town and examined the heads of all the clergymen in the place and "found us all deficient in the organ of reverence." They all admitted that none of them were especially gifted with natural piety or love of worship. He told them, "You have all mistaken your calling. You ought not to be ministers."

I'm not sure things have changed that much in the one hundred fifty years since he wrote that. Too many of us are typically full of ambition for God, but we are not reverent before God, and the irreverence before God has its corollary in an irreverence of congregations.

This leads to the insight—developed in so many of its facets by Berry—that the more local life is, the more intense, more colorful, more rich because it has limits. These limits, instead of being interpreted as limitations to be broken through, are treasured as boundaries to respect. No farmer looks on his or her fences as restrictions to be broken down or broken through as a sign of progress. A fence is a border, defining the place. When I know what is mine, I know also what is not mine and can live as a neighbor.

This has immense implications for my work. For one thing, it locates my work in what I can actually do among the people for whom I have primary responsibility. For several decades now, under the influence of the myth of progress and in ignorance of craft, the term "pastor" has been a gunny sack into which all sorts of tinker's damns have been thrown. In my early years I was running all over town from committee to committee, conference to conference, organization to organization, doing all manner of good work, scattering seed in everybody's field but my own. I now know that I was doing all that because it seemed more important than the humble task I was given in my own congregation: more urgent, and certainly more noticeable. When I disciplined myself to my congregation, I found something far better.

An understanding of limit is also a prophylaxis against mistaking religious cancer for spiritual growth. In the consumerist/ecclesiastical economy I grew up in, I evaluated progress in terms of larger numbers. I paid attention only to those parts of reality that I could measure with numbers. I got used to using the word growth in this context.

But growth, and Berry was my primary teacher in this, is a biological, not an arithmetical, metaphor. Growth in biology has to do with timing, passivity, waiting, and maturity. There is a proper size to each thing. There are proportions to be attended to. It is an exceedingly complex and mysterious thing, this process of growth. Every congregation has proportions, symmetries, and a size proper to it. Erwin Chargaff once commented that our country has always had a tendency to blow up every balloon until it bursts. He went on to comment: "We have lost entirely this sense of measure, of reticence, of knowing one's own boundaries. Man is only strong when he is conscious of his own weakness. Otherwise, the eagles of heaven will eat his liver, as Prometheus found out. No eagle of heaven any more. No Prometheus: now we get cancer instead—the prime disease of advanced civilizations."

Along the way I noticed that the individuals most obsessed with the numerical aspects of growth are, typically, our adolescents. When I was fifteen, I enrolled with a couple of my friends in a mail-order bodybuilding course. Every week we got out the tape measures and wrote down the statistics on our swelling biceps, our thickening thighs, our chest expansion. The girls, I later learned, were going through similar exercises, measuring their breasts.

One sign of maturity is a loss of interest in these kinds of numbers. So why is there still so much adolescent measuring of religious biceps and breasts in American churches? Lines in a Norman Dubie poem give the lie to our ecclesiastical obsession with number: "With fractions as the bottom integer gets bigger, Mother, it / Represents less."

I'll give Peter Forsyth the last word: "You have but a corner of the vineyard, and cannot appeal to all men [and women]; humility is a better equipment than ambition, even the ambition of doing much good."

6

Troy, Betty Crocker, and Mother Mary

Reflections on Gender and Ambition

Jeanne Murray Walker

WE PULL ON KHAKI safari hats and dodge across the highway. It's ten in the morning and already heat is hammering down from the heavens. Heat radiates up from the macadam. Even the cracked and broken earth smells parched. I try to think of a graceful way of turning back. What kind of craziness is this, to climb all day on these stones in temperatures well over a hundred degrees? We have come to the Aegean Coast to see ancient cities, the place, for example, where Menelaus fought the Trojans and reclaimed his stolen wife. Helen of Troy.

This is a landscape in which to ponder ambition.

A wooden, ten-story replica of the Trojan Horse towers above us. It looks like a clumsy rocking horse or child's drawing, built grotesquely large. It represents the extravagant gift the Greeks left outside the gates of Troy. If the Trojans had guessed it was a hoax, they might have massacred the Greek fighters who hovered inside, and then the history of Troy would be different. But the oblivious Trojans rolled the Greek horse into their city. They must have been flattered: even the mighty Greeks admired their city.

We stare at a plaque as mournful as a tombstone: ILIOS/WILUSA. In the tongue of its own day, it speaks the name of the fallen city. Then we slog around a several-mile loop, climbing the ruins of the walls of the nine different Troys built on this site. Since the path is uneven, all morning we halt and stumble in the ferocious heat. The chiseled white stones that once comprised the walls of Troy lie scattered around us like toys. We talk softly about Priam, Hector, Paris, Ulysses, Menelaus, Agamemnon. We bring to life the men who built Troy, the men who burned it. Under a fury of sun we trudge on and on through the rubble, pondering ambition and fame. How quickly it vanishes. Zip. And what remains?

Memento Mori.

Finally we sit down at a picnic table in the shade, where Cemil, our lovely guide informs us that there was no Helen. Not really. What the Greeks wanted, according to archeologists, was neither the most beautiful woman in the world nor revenge on Paris, the man who stole her. The Greeks wanted bronze. And they wanted a sea port.

At Cemil's subtraction of Helen—his demythologizing of the story—I feel pain around my heart. In one blow this ravages not only the poems of Homer and Virgil, but the work of poets like Tennyson and Yeats who staked their fame on the old stories. I wonder, what else has to go? I am mentally tossing out *The Oresteia* and operas, too, like *Dido and Aeneas*, when one of us mentions that a certain kind of truth lies beyond history. Or something like that. Surely the old stories are true at a more transcendent level, we tell each other wistfully.

It's not until I arrive back home that I think, Wait! There must have been women in Troy, I mean women who were not Helen. How could I have forgotten? At first I feel embarrassed, puzzled. After a lifetime of work and arranging day care and juggling household duties, I should remember the women. As I think about this in the following weeks, it seems to me that I have betrayed my life, my own experience. And then I began to feel bereft at the loss women, at my lost chance to envision them there at Troy. I feel remorse at my carelessness. If I can't remember there were women, how can I expect historians to remember them?

In the old poems, women are mostly incidental: the model of a good wife, Penelope, for instance, and the mad prophet, Cassandra, and the outraged Medea. And then there were a whole variety of seductresses. The trouble is, none of these women are us. I don't identify with them; most women don't. How could we? They are not the protagonists. They are not at the center of the old stories. And after all, readers, including women, feel the joys and sorrows and rage and tenderness mainly of protagonists, that is to say, men. We keep our eyes trained on the men.

So here I am, writing this essay, remembering myself as I was last summer, standing there in the plain, hot rubble of Troy, and the Acropolis and

Ephesus, forgetting the women—all except for the exquisite Helen. And now, apparently, Helen has been kicked away from the center of the story by archeologists. For weeks after seeing Troy I wonder who those women at Troy were. I ponder their ambition. I ponder ambition itself. What does it mean? How has it affected my own story?

As a girl, I was powerfully affected by my mother's ambition, which was shaped by her difficult life and by the American culture around us. Moreover, I suspect that my ambition has been imprinted on my children, though it is harder to say exactly how. I have been pondering how that word, *ambition*, echoes down generations and how it means something different for men than it does for women.

⭤

Ambition. For me, the word is ambiguous. It is a chameleon.

Put a chameleon on a leaf and it turns green. Lower it to the brick patio and it tints toward rust. Lift it to the white siding of your house and, to oblige, it bleaches itself.

Not many English words are as versatile as *ambition*. Think of it as the eggplant of the language. Pair it with any other food and it takes on their taste: onions, mozzarella, tomatoes, garlic.

If you want, you can think of ambition as a form of greed. Hence the sentence: *watch out for him; he's an ambitious so-and-so and he'll cut you off at the pass*. But let's face it, without ambition, it's impossible to get anywhere. You might as well try driving a U-Haul with no gas. My Minnesota relatives favored ambition. They nicknamed it *get-up-and-go*, as in *she doesn't have much get-up-and-go*. In fact they worried because I spent so much time sitting in a chair, reading. My mother used to tell me that I was lazy. I had no get-up-and-go.

⭤

It was my mother's ambition for her children to have ambition.

When I was in my early twenties, though my mother didn't know it, I was gripped by the need to Do Something Important. Not that I was sure of what to do. It was the early seventies. The seams of the world had already split open. Many of us had protested about civil rights. Then came the assassinations. Between them, we strode with banners down the wide avenues of Chicago protesting the Vietnam War. We stopped traffic and made obscene gestures at the police. We huddled in rallies and gave press conferences about how we were going to dump Lyndon Johnson. And we won at least part of what we wanted. But beneath my own political action, I felt nagging skepticism. Our moralizings about the older generation sometimes sounded to me like self-righteous cant. Calamity threw its shadows all around us, and it was not easy to figure out what to do. My confusion made me feel that it was all the more urgent to do something fast.

The Baptist church where I was reared (all day Sunday and Wednesday night prayer meeting, as well as Vacation Bible School, revivals, and holidays) had pounded into me the fleeting nature of time. *Work, for the night is coming*, thrummed in my brain no matter what I was doing, like a heavy beat under a melody. *Work, for the night is coming!*

The brevity and seriousness of life was underscored by the death of my father when I was thirteen. He suffered with a terminal heart condition. Five years earlier, specialists had given him the option: he might live for as long as three years, they predicted. Or he could elect to have immediate surgery to attempt to correct the problem, but he had a fifty percent chance of dying on the operating table.

The pressure for a choice, the high stakes, his bad odds, and above all, my inability to do anything to fix it, churned in me. He decided not to have surgery. He wanted the certainty of at least some more time with us kids. He grew sicker. Both my mother and father acted with great courage. They set about getting my mother ready to support the family.

I learned the value of action. I learned that women need to find some way of supporting themselves and their children. Since I had already experienced success as a writer, I skewed off to graduate school to earn a PhD in English. I had felt the power of words and books. I believed then—and I still believe—that books can change the world.

Around the time I began writing my dissertation, I had my first child. I was just beginning to realize that I would be peeling a lot of potatoes for the rest of my days. I didn't understand this until so late because, since emerging into adulthood, I had been living the sheltered life of a student. Ideas reign supreme in universities; the cafeteria makes the meals.

By contrast, I now found myself drowning in details. Everything we owned, every single spoon and paper clip, had just passed through my hands twice—I had packed and unpacked it to move. And then there was the dailyness of taking care of another human body—the diapers, the stroller, the playpen, the sanitizer, the bottles, the special implements for washing and drying the bottles, the lamby she couldn't do without, and on and on. I was beginning to realize that, by marrying and becoming a mother, I had emerged as The Keeper of Things. I was dumbfounded by all the stuff and bereft of words to explain myself, since I seemed to be living a normal, even happy American life. Uneventful as my life must have seemed to others, every day I awoke to a minor crisis. I didn't complain much; I felt it would have been childish to grouse about the details. After all, someone has to wash the dishes (although it certainly seemed odd that I was washing dishes every time I turned around). I was grimly determined to become efficient, to learn how to get the details over with quickly and then move on to Something Important.

The Something Important turned out to be writing poetry.

Poetry?

I know. I know.

These days American poetry has gone hip. Poetry wears a steel nose ring and sports pink hair, or at least not the same color hair as it had last night. She postures on stage, gyrating and slamming vocabulary together, then spitting it all into a mike. She offers to those of us in the audience a regular rodeo of daredevil, death-defying tricks and tarted-up rhymes.

History will decide the value of this kind of poetry.

I aspire to something more plain, more like Homer. When we were in Turkey, I gazed upon the debris of a sports stadium and an ancient market place at the Acropolis of Pergamum. Rubble strewn everywhere. But open *The Odyssey* and you can see a ship slowly pulling up to shore. You feel oars dragging against the heavy, bright water. You hear the shouts of men as they unfold their limbs from their long ride and leap onto the sand. You smell grass and notice dust motes spinning in sunlight. Homer's poetry has kept the ancient world alive to us.

My ambition is to write poetry that defeats time.

᳍

In 1921, the company that later became General Mills invented Betty Crocker. By the 1950s, this marketing device had become the most famous woman in America. At that time, most women didn't work outside the home (that is, unless their husbands had died). Moreover, to relieve them of housework they enjoyed an embarrassment of labor-saving devices. A

Betty Crocker cake mix is, in fact, a labor-saving device, but not one like a vacuum cleaner or a dish washer. It offers women a task that is minimal, but which they can be applauded for accomplishing. A woman has to add a couple of eggs and water to the mix, beat it into batter, pour it into a cake pan, and voila! she can turn out a "homemade" cake for dinner. Women loved the illusion of labor; in fact, simpler, one-step cake mixes didn't sell. Eventually the shrewd Betty Crocker wrote a whole cookbook based on the principle: follow a few simple steps, sit back, and rake in the credit. Our family's edition of the *Betty Crocker Cook Book* portrays a well-groomed, very together lady hosting a barbecue on her back lawn where her husband is doing the grilling.

It was during the Betty Crocker era that I was trying to grasp what it meant to be a woman. I concluded that a woman was a Not-Man. For instance, a woman was like the fabric left after I cut the pattern to sew a dress. Imagine blue plaid fabric laid out on the floor. I would cluster the pattern pieces carefully at one end so the leftover fabric would be as large and useful as possible. The leftovers I made into hot pads, shoulder pads, doll dresses, and sachets, all things I didn't want or need. It was the dress I cared about.

I kept aspiring to be the dress rather than the leftover random shape.

Which is why at nine or ten I aspired to become a shortstop. Sentenced to bed by eight p.m. on spring evenings, I was seduced beneath my tent of covers by the golden voice of Jack Hyland calling play-by-play for the Lincoln Chiefs on KOLN. I imagined Ollie Anderson and Norm Brown and Vance Carlson and the whole roster of guys at Sherman Park. I visualized their tics, their mysterious handshakes with one another, their bus trips, their good luck charms. At school, I lived for the baseball we played during recess and lunch. I loved standing in the batter's box, defying the pitcher, assessing the mood of the opposing team, waiting for the slight breeze and whistle of the ball over the plate. I adored pulling the bat, hearing the solid crack of wood, feeling the shock of the impact from my wrist to my shoulder. I believed that I was destined to play baseball just like my grandfather who was the shortstop for the Yankton, South Dakota, farm team.

By the age of twelve, I finally noticed that only men played professional baseball. Harboring the ambition to be a shortstop was like deciding that I had a future as an eagle. I failed to realize that I didn't have wings.

Once I got the idea that I should aim at what a girl might actually do, I kept my eyes on the high school girls who wore sweater sets and pearls.

They might have been cheerleaders or maybe class secretaries. But for sure they were not the football star or the class president. They were polite and they modulated their voices. They were drifting into the arms of Betty Crocker. Humdrum was in vogue. Families named their dogs Lassie and Spot. Mamie Eisenhower was First Lady. *Good Housekeeping* and *Ladies Home Journal* were written and edited by men to instruct women about how to keep a nice house. There were no women radio hosts or news broadcasters, no female faces on money. I wanted to love God and be His child, but there were no women deacons or ministers at our church, either. A brief review of the literature reveals that Snow White slept through the decade of her adolescence, tended by seven dwarves. Then she woke to the smooch of a man who offered her a perfect life, which, however, is missing from the story. Ditto Sleeping Beauty. And think of all the evil stepmothers in the fairy tales. Consider, also, the rhymes, the adages. *Boys will be boys. Jill came tumbling after. Frightened Miss Muffett away.*

↢↣

It's the mid-1980s, summer, and I am once again packing wipes and teething biscuits into a diaper bag to go to the zoo or to Fairmont Park or to the West Philly pool with a two-year-old. I am making him sandwiches without crusts, wiping his nose, rolling a ball back and forth with him, changing his diapers, getting groceries, cleaning the kitchen cupboards while he bangs pans and pots on the floor beside me. Day after day, I perform the eternally recurring tasks of a mother: picking up his dropped toys, slowing my pace to match his tiny, wandering steps, giving him sticky hugs, shaping his sweaty blond hair after his nap, nursing him in a darkened room, telling him stories and jokes.

With this child, as with my first, I learn to relax into blissful, cyclical, repetitive time.

But occasionally in the middle of this bliss, the thought crosses my mind that soon I will need to go back to teaching. I see swift and dangerous linear time slashing through the summer like a highway through a sunny meadow. I hear the fast traffic. I awake to the shock of people going places; my colleagues, my friends, the others. People who are writing books, making deals, healing the sick, preaching sermons, getting elected. I am newly puzzled by this awakening. Why don't they relax? I conclude that ambition is the fuel driving their cars. I look around our house for my ambition, but it is missing. I ponder how to recover it.

During Jack's nap that afternoon, I sit down at my desk. Propelled by desperation, I catch the updraft of an idea so powerful that it spills quickly into several poems I see might begin a series.

Yesterday, that happened.

Today I am alert, following the scent of that idea to find out where it will go. This ambition isn't a drive for power in the world. It feels more like a journey driven by curiosity. It's about eleven in the morning and Philadelphia is suffering a heat wave, and Jack and I are hanging out on the second floor where there's no air conditioner. But *Sesame Street* is rocking on TV and Jack is crazy about *Sesame Street*, one of two programs he is allowed to watch. He's sitting on the old blue couch. For three minutes he gnaws thoughtfully on a graham cracker, focusing on Big Bird. I am sitting at a makeshift desk behind him, trying to stalk the poems I started yesterday.

Suddenly Jack reels back to me for comfort. He buries his head in my lap and I lift him up to tickle him. We are both hot, stripped down to shorts and T-shirts. Plastic toys in primary colors are scattered around us like the rubble of Troy. Jack scampers back to watch more *Sesame Street*. I turn to my computer, which I have to boot up every time I turn it on and which has already conked out twice, sending yesterday's poems into oblivion. I am desperate to remember them, to build on them, to get somewhere, to find traction.

But in the background I hear Fredericke von Stade singing the alphabet song. Then clunk! Jack's plastic cup spills and milk runs all over the place. I know it will drip down onto the dining room ceiling below. I can envision a stain spreading on the plaster down there. I race for a towel.

I return to the computer, but I can feel myself sliding backwards, unable to remember yesterday's beautiful vision. I feel my life disappearing. Time is pulling away like a train that I have failed to catch. My history is being written and this is it. I hear my colleagues in the distance, surging forward. All I have left is this beautiful child. I would not change places with anybody. I am fortunate, I am lucky, I am crazy about him. I would give my life for him, but please, God, not my morning. Not this last morning before I have to go back to teaching.

I try to buck up my determination. I will concentrate. I go back to the computer, boot it again, listen for the faintest updraft, the slightest whiff of language that visited me yesterday. But I get an error message on the computer. I pull the manual from a bookshelf and page through it, unable to focus or settle. In the background I hear the letter Q talking to Big Bird about all the words that begin with Q.

Eventually I give up. Jack crawls onto my lap, and I carry him over to the blue couch where we sit together and watch Maria. She is wooing Oscar, the Grouch from behind his garbage can, charming him into a full-blown conversation. Oscar, comma, the Grouch. The boisterous Comma is today's most magnetic personality on *Sesame Street*. Jack relaxes, leans into me. We laugh. Who knows how much he understands or why he is happy.

I think he's happy because I am at peace. I have been the grouch in our neighborhood. I repent. For the millionth time, I give up ambition. It is heaven to give up ambition and just sit on the blue couch with my child.

For thirty years I spun in this kind of loop. My ambition to write seemed impossible to attain because of the strange universe I entered when I agreed to be a mother. But of course when I assented to become a mother, I had no idea I was entering a strange world. The choice I made that Tuesday morning, to watch *Sesame Street* with Jack rather than to write—can it be called a choice?—has defined me. Now that I'm in my 60s, I realize that my bibliography reflects thousands of such choices. I also know that some men are doing the same kind of parenting these days and taking the same kinds of hits at work. How many men do this kind of parenting, I don't know, but I praise them. I praise all the grown-up men who play ball with their children and coach their children's teams and help their children with homework.

But there will always be a difference between the way men and women parent. Women shed IQ points during pregnancy and lactation. That doesn't just appear to be happening. It really happens. It has been documented.

My mother was wrong. I *was* ambitious. Maybe it was the very act of her telling me I had no ambition that kindled my ambition. I wonder. In any case, I am grateful to her for being concerned enough to talk about it. The truth is, once I understood that writing was my calling, I wrote. I did sound and meter exercises. I improvised. I practiced. I revised. I was usually at my computer by eight in the morning and often I was still there at six at night. That is, until I had children.

I did not grasp the power of those children to mesmerize and bewitch. Better to underestimate a riptide. I was hijacked by hormones, wild with love. I doubt that I was unusual. Much of the time I felt joy, but it was not all joy, this mothering. It was the midnight feedings, catching the child as he tumbled off ladder-back chairs, feeling in the pit of my stomach his smashed finger. I was thrilled by the terror of failing a tiny being who has no one else in the world to keep him alive. When the astonishing, bright new creation runs into the street, you follow him into traffic to snatch him to safety. You just do. It is unthinkable that this child who has been entrusted to you should be destroyed on your watch. The mystery is that there are so few songs written about this kind of mother-love, no epic poems honoring this kind of timeless, cyclical childbearing and childrearing.

⊝

But we do have the story of the Virgin Mary and we have the prodigious Madonnas of the Renaissance. The summer our family went to Florence, I saw hundreds of versions of the Madonna with Child in the Uffizi. They are gorgeous and formal and composed, most of them. They became a proof subject for Florentine painters who were ambitious for patrons and fame. I stood before those paintings, grateful to be eavesdropping on the living, timeless rapport of Mother and Child. They embodied the Platonic thing, the big, true narrative to which my own mothering life referred: the narrative about Mary. If she had ambitions before Gabriel arrived, she surrendered them when she gave the avuncular angel her answer. *"Let it be unto me as you have said,"* she told him, pitching herself into mothering time. Yes, she said. I will live this life you have proposed.

And that takes care of that. Except she had no idea what would happen to her or to her child.

Michelangelo's *Pieta* reveals where that *yes* took her. The grief and love that saturates Mary's face as she holds her dead son shakes me to the core—and maybe other viewers, too—partly because I felt such loss as our children grew and left us. Hers is the knowing look, the glance of the mother who has surrendered herself and her body to another, and who is now giving him up. She is forcing herself to stay in the present tense, to hold the weight of her grown-up son suddenly ripped from her in such a hideous way.

In Istanbul we visited the Chora Church, a church rebuilt in the twelfth century and dedicated to Mary. On its walls her life unfolds in luminous and nuanced fourteenth-century mosaics. Byzantine Christians spoke of Mary as the container of the uncontainable. They thought of her as the box that contained the Word, the Ark that held the covenant, the body that sheltered

God. Mary was those things; we aren't—the rest of us who first contain and then mother our children. But we do experience the alchemy of life growing within us, the mysterious identities of the beings we are given, and the strange weightlessness of repetitive, cyclical time. Months pass and the children change and we begin to see them as if they were cubist paintings, simultaneously as babies, as children, as teenagers, as grown-ups. So Mary, holding her grown-up son, might be simultaneously thinking of the baby, the child, the young teenager. The Gospel of Luke tells us that Mary kept all these things and pondered them in her heart.

My friend William Griffin once regaled me with the story that before Gabriel spoke to Mary, he had asked other women to become the mother of God. They said no. They were too busy. They were afraid. They had other ambitions. I wondered how many of them had turned Gabriel down. It is a paradox that by surrendering her ambitions, Mary became the most famous mother of all, the most often portrayed woman in history.

⟿

If I had been asked by Gabriel to become God's mother, I think I'd have demurred too. It was a freak request, without precedent, offering not one solitary prototype for a woman to follow. I modified but did not surrender my own ambitions when I had children, and I often wonder how my children have suffered because of that. You have heard this question asked until it now seems threadbare. *Can a woman have everything*? How much time is enough for a child? Can a mother who is often distracted by work give a child enough attention? How does a mother's ambition imprint her child?

How can anyone know?

But I can tell you stories.

Jack is twelve and it's Saturday morning, and on my list of chores is driving him to the Academy of Music. He has an audition to play a Hayden piece with the Philadelphia orchestra.

Around nine, he gets up and wanders downstairs, bleary-eyed. I bribe him to eat breakfast. I will make him pancakes, I say. He grins but refuses the offer. Then he strolls into the dining room, gets out his fiddle, tucks it under his chin, and eases into the Hayden. I wander in and out of the dining room, pulling out linens for the twelve people who are coming to dinner that night, noticing how lanky Jack has become, tousle-haired, neat-fingered, tan, looking more like an athlete than a musician.

He has played the violin since he was six. He has become a prodigy. This is a fact of our lives now, but it seems a remarkable coincidence. Before I turned to writing poetry, I played the violin. Some days I practiced for six hours; I won awards, but I was nowhere nearly as gifted as he is. Never on a day of his life has he practiced for six hours and still, he's better at twelve than I was at eighteen. I consider whether this is good or bad. Jack probably feels the weight of difficult choice: to live up to the overblown predictions about his future or to feel like a failure.

I listen to the cicadas outside the window, wondering whether my own ambition to play the violin leapfrogged into my child. I imagine the maniac who asked Jesus, please, to get the demon out of him. I picture somewhere in Jack's head a tiny me, scrubbing away at scales and arpeggios. I'm not kidding. This vision is terrifying. It keeps me awake for whole nights. I wonder whether my son has been visited with the misfortune of my violin ambition.

Except that I never wanted him to play the violin. At least sometimes, when I'm thinking straight, I understand that how a mother passes on her ambition is much more complicated than that.

Here's what happened. When Jack was four, his father's sister, Jane, and her family visited us in Philadelphia. Charlie, Jack's cousin, was about seven at the time. He had outgrown his sixteenth-size violin and Janie brought it as a present for Jack. Why sell it back to the store, she asked, since she would get only a few dollars for it.

At some point during our conversation, I picked up the tiny thing, took it to another room, and played it. It sounded tinny, like most student violins, but still, it was a perfectly formed miniature. To me its arrival seemed almost providential. Later, while I served dinner and we talked and ate, the violin sat on the coffee table, radiating charisma. I kept ducking into the living room to check on it, its reddish wood, its tiny black pegs, the little bridge holding up its strings.

When John and Janie and their two kids left, Jack wanted to play with his new violin, but he was only four, and it wasn't long before he was banging it against the floor. I couldn't bear to watch him smash it, even though it was his. So his father and I explained to him that we needed to save the instrument for him till he was older. We wrapped it in flannel, laid it in its case, and tucked it into our linen closet. He watched. We promised him that we would take it out whenever he wanted, and hold it. If he still wanted to play it when he was six, I promised that I would find him a teacher.

The violin became the apple in the garden that Jack was not permitted to eat. Almost every day he asked for it and we took it down for him. Two years later, on his sixth birthday, surrounded by a party's worth of kids and a slagheap of presents, he cocked his head, squinted up at me, and said, *"Now I get to play my violin!"*

That was early June. I dragged my feet finding a teacher. I knew what an evil instrument the violin could be, how whiny and out of tune it could sound. Nevertheless, Jack kept pestering me. In the end, I just asked a neighbor for the name of the woman who gave her son Suzuki lessons.

In a year-and-a-half Jack tore through six levels of Suzuki, and then his teacher admitted that he was beyond her. She needed to hand him off to her own master teacher. Jack auditioned with Lee Snyder, a Philadelphia violin guru with a national reputation who was later to become esteemed in our house almost as a saint.

After Jack auditioned for Lee, Lee gravely confided that Jack was very gifted, but that he was being hampered by an incorrect bow hold. I would need to bring him several days a week for half-hour tutorials until this could be corrected.

Really? For an incorrect bow hold? More than once a week? To Jenkintown? Count it up. That's almost eight hours a week.

And I would need to practice with Jack an hour a day, Lee continued.

An hour? Every day?

Yes.

That's a total of fifteen hours a week gone from my writing time.

The very tall, slender Lee, who was excited by Jack's talent, stood waiting for my reply, expecting that I would just naturally supply whatever Jack needed. It was a crossroads, a moment of choice, a potential disaster.

My mind wandered like a truant to the ill-fated string quartet that serenaded passengers on the Titanic as it hit the iceberg. I envisioned strains of Mozart calming the darting, panicked passengers. Then I watched the first violinist's elegant bowing as he slipped beneath fathoms of water. The lovely music, like the last light, was extinguished.

Meanwhile, Lee was paging through his date book. He said, "I have time at four o'clock this Monday, at seven o'clock on Wednesday, and around three o'clock on Friday. Could you bring him then?"

"Okay," I said.

My voice was a whisper, a pale ghost. But I did say yes. And that is how our family embarked upon the kind of intense training reserved for Olympic athletes and a small group of young musicians in this country.

An eight-year-old, of course, doesn't naturally hightail it home from school to practice. Oh, the first couple of weeks Jack did. Then his attention flagged. I figured that meant he was choosing not to practice.

Fine, I thought. Good. He's making a decision. Let's be done with this. Maybe I'll finally be able to write poetry again.

But really. He loved his lessons. He was crazy about Lee. Whenever I reminded him, he quickly picked up his fiddle. So I reluctantly started nudging him to practice.

But then who was driving this music? I worried. I rummaged for the beating heart of it. Whose idea was this, anyway? *Whose ambition*?

I didn't know. I still don't.

At the Academy of Music, Jack was given high marks for the Hayden. He placed, but he didn't win. Two years later, he auditioned again, this time with the Kabalevsky. In the Green Room that morning all the mothers seemed to be wearing immaculate pink Gucci suits and patent leather heels. I thought that the mothers must have known one another and had planned appropriate outfits. I didn't know any of them. Moreover, I needed to shop for the dinner for twelve people that would happen at our house that night. I hadn't even considered what to wear. I was wearing thrift-shop jeans and a T-shirt. I wondered whether Jack noticed, whether he cared, whether it would skew his chances. I felt that I had let him down. I did not own a designer suit, but that wasn't the point. I had not considered his audition an important enough event to dress up for.

As we waited for the kids to be called to their auditions, the mothers groomed their children apprehensively. The teenagers were gifted musicians who propped sheet music on the furniture, stood back, and shouldered their fiddles. They reeled off the most difficult passages from the Mendelssohn, the Brahms, the Barber, the Bruch.

I spied Hilary Hahn, who must have been about sixteen, crumpled in a corner, intently drilling into a paperback copy of *Great Expectations*. I had been invited to be a visiting poet in one of Hahn's classes at the Curtis Institute, so I knew that her imagination is almost equally as engaged with words as it is with music. When Curtis accepted her as a student at the age of ten, so the gossip goes, her father moved with her to Philadelphia, rented an apartment, and supported her rise to a remarkable career as a soloist.

Thinking of my own life and that of my child, I wondered whether her career was fueled by her own ambition or her father's.

But who can tell?

And anyway, that's another story.

Jack played the Tchaikovsky with the Lansdowne Symphony Orchestra and soloed with several other adult orchestras before he graduated from high school. Then he went off to study at the Oberlin College Conservatory on a Dean's scholarship. At the college he signed up for a course in political science and fell in love with politics. He finished a politics degree, went to law school, became a district attorney, and is now a litigator in a law firm.

I don't grieve over the fact that my child doesn't play the violin any more. I don't play the violin either. I write.

I'm guessing that the way we mothers pass ambition to our children escapes charts and graphs. Maybe the ironies and paradoxes of the way we transfer our longings and aspirations can only be registered in stories and poems. Read the mind-boggling narratives in Genesis, for example, about how a mother's ambition can drive her children and their children and, in turn, theirs. The ambitious Rebekah, who favors her second son, Jacob, dresses him up to resemble his older brother, Esau, and coaches him about how to steal Esau's birthright. Jacob and his wives, Rachael and Leah, as well as his older brother, Esau, live out the consequences of Rebekah's ambition.

My mother, who was ambitious for her children, who was relieved and happy that my teenage reading did not destroy me but flowered into a lifetime of happy work, gave me a sign to put on my desk at the university. She wrongly believed that sign summarized what was most important to me: Dr. Jeanne Walker. She thought the degree mattered more than it did. Because she herself was not a reader, she never really understood why I wanted to write. For a while I buried her gift in one of my drawers. But recently to honor the ambition which shaped my mother's children, I have taken it out. Now I keep it on my desk where I can see it.

7

Dreams Are Dangerous; They Uncover Your Bones

Diane Glancy

I LOOKED UP THE definition of ambition in my *Webster's New World Dictionary*. It means, to go about. The dictionary then adds, to get votes. Ambition comes from the Latin, *ambitio*—a going around. The dictionary also said to see ambient, which means—to go around—surrounding—on all sides. I like the definition of ambition. Ambition is everywhere—on every side of my life. It is all around my writing. I would have been wiped out if it wasn't for ambition.

Writing is an arduous task. It takes going around to all sides to gather whatever information the piece requires. It takes ambition to stick with the piece especially when it feels like it isn't going anywhere. For me, it takes many drafts to reach the final one. There are many rejections of the manuscript as well as the individual pieces I send out as the manuscript-in-progress taking shape. I would be discouraged if it wasn't for ambition. I want my work to be what it was imagined in my head. I want to see the finished piece shined and polished. Ready for market. Fattened as a little pig.

I would like to think that ambition is a gift if looked at from a Christian perspective. It seems to me that God was ambitious when He made the world and all that is in it. His plans for us are ambitious. He sees us redeemed to Himself—worshipping Him in this life and for eternity. How amazing—creatures who follow the flesh can, by His power of transformation, be made into spiritual beings—saints actually. That is ambition!

Was not Christ ambitious when He went to the cross? His act would redeem mankind—or those who believed on His name. It is a message that is not accepted by everyone, of course, though His ambition is for everyone to come to the Father through Him.

Was it not ambitious of Moses to think the people could cross the Red Sea? Maybe it was more not having a choice. But he stood on ambition. He took the initiative. He held up his staff and the water parted. When Pharaoh's horses went into the sea, the waters closed over them, but the Israelites walked through the sea on dry ground (Exod 15:19). Was not Miriam ambitious as she sang her song on the other shore?—"Sing to the Lord for he has triumphed gloriously, horse and rider he has thrown into the sea" (Exod 15:20–21 RSV).

In the Old Testament, Solomon was the king of ambition, writing thousands of sayings, building a magnificent temple and a more magnificent house. Ambition was in the structure of his bones. In the New Testament, the Apostle Paul is his equivalent, though he had no earthly wealth. Look at his unending journeys in the book of Acts. His efforts were Solomonesque.

As a Christian, my personal ambition is to belong to God. I want my name in God's book—the book that Christ is worthy to open at the end of this age. To me, that is the ultimate ambition.

For a writer, temporal ambition also is vital. Ambition causes a necessary self-promotion. You need self-promotion when you are writing a book. You tell yourself you can do it. You need self-promotion when you send your manuscript out. You need self-promotion when you get it back. You keep going and going, and finally there's a publisher for your work. Then you have to self-promote the book, giving readings, giving talks. You self-promote to get your work out there once you've self-promoted yourself into writing the book. Is there another way?

The first reference for ambition in my thesaurus is intention. Intentionality. Purpose. Plan. Resolve. Determination. Motive. Tenacity. All those words my work-ethic, goal-oriented parents used. Ambition is the intended. The thought-out plan. It is the opposite of chance.

Ambition also is listed under desire in the thesaurus. Like words are longing, hankering, yearning, coveting, craving, concupiscence, aspiration, eagerness, zeal, ardor, solicitude, anxiety, sheep eyes. So there is a negative—in the sense of going out to get votes for the sole purpose of getting votes. Maybe I should warn myself about selfishness here.

⊖

Yet, of course, I want publication. Who teaches and does not know the importance of publication? It means promotion. It means tenure. It is substantiation for one's existence in an academic field. I have known literature scholars who did not consider creative writing a legitimate discipline. But publication seemed to ameliorate that objection, on the surface anyway. Publication certainly is a large part of one's progress in academia, along with strong student evaluations and an active presence in the institution. When I was up for tenure, I wrote an eleven-page letter explaining why I should receive it. It was full of ambition. I recounted past achievements. Present activities. My five-year plan of what was still ahead. There is no room for humility in a tenure-review case.

The University of North Dakota is in the process of collecting my papers. I have not been paid for them. I send them whatever I have ready. I pile up the drafts from whatever manuscript will be published. I send them my rejection notes. I send them acceptances and my flyers for talks, readings, and lectures. I have been ambitious. I have been going about. Why should I be embarrassed to feel this? What else can I do but write? I have to make it count. But why should every word of mine be saved, flagged, and touted? Why can't I refrain from mentioning this? Excuse my ambition. Excuse me while I try to excuse myself.

There are warnings against ambition in the Bible. According to James, where jealousy and selfish ambition exist, there will be disorder and every vile practice (3:16 RSV). Where envying and strife are, there is confusion and every evil work (3:14 KJV). The modifier, selfish, is there in the Revised Standard Version of the Bible.

Yet self is important to me. At times, I felt it was all I had. I am not a selfless person. I am not unselfish. I have had to make my own way, with the help of Christ, of course. My life of ambition has been blessed and it has been thwarted. I have had to learn patience. I once heard Richard Foster say that ambition has no patience, and I recognized the truth of that statement.

⌁

The Apostle Paul had ambition for the believers to grow up in Christ. Why else would he write all those letters that fill the New Testament? Does he ever let up or change his tune as he pleads for a transformation of ambition into the ultimate transformation—that of an ambition for the things of God? I belong to two Bible study groups. I read God's word. I have ambition to be the kind of Christian I understand the Bible to mean. I have ambition to be around people who like to talk about God.

I have ambition to continue the course of my life. At one time, I had to publish in my field of native studies, but since I have retired I want to write about faith. My agent and the presses that have published my native work are not interested. I have to begin again to find a way to publish this new body of my work. It will come with faith, patience, and ambition. It will come when the work is ready.

Where does anyone get the audacity to experiment and stretch out where they have not gone previously? In my opinion, it takes ambition to do that. I tell myself, I've already written in a certain way. Now, reach out. How could I try something new if not for ambition? Ambition tempered with reason, of course. Ambition fueled by faith along a fitting channel.

⌁

Ambition causes me to persevere. I still have one project to finish that involves native voices. It's about the history of Native American education. I have worked on it for several years, exploring different venues to carry the story. First-person narrative. Or third-person. My publisher asked me to put my own voice into it as well. So I am writing about the process of writing and how it uncovered my own school experiences. The manuscript is nonfiction as well as a fictional historical narrative, a created narrative of sorts titled *Fort Marion Prisoners and the Trauma of Native Education*. It is about the 1875–78 Fort Marion prisoners sent from Indian Territory to St. Augustine, Florida, at the end of the Plains Indians wars. There, the prisoners were educated and Christianized—some of them anyway, thus the title. To live in this world, one must be educated, but to be educated, one loses a part of oneself.

What was it like—that great upheaval—that view of the ocean for the first time? My own education also was an upheaval. I keep twisting and bending the narrative of the manuscript-in-progress until I can follow it through without snagging. One native who read the manuscript said that it was too passive. He wanted it more militant. After all, the Indians were POWs at Fort Marion. But I didn't want their protest as much as their assimilation into another culture that included ledger-book drawings and life-casts that are housed at the Peabody Museum at Harvard. I wanted to focus on the growth of literacy. I am responsible for the way I see the story, or the way the story came to me over the many ambitious attempts to capture it.

After working further on the manuscript, I have another box ready to send the library at the University of North Dakota. In it are previous drafts of *Fort Marion Prisoners* and notes I took during various trips to Fort Sill in Lawton, Oklahoma (the starting point), to St. Augustine, Florida (the destination). Printouts of historical information. Brochures from Fort Marion. Shells from the beach. Copies of pages of historical books and reports. Papers and papers from the Internet. Notes from the books I've read.

Ambition continues to run everywhere like the air. I have ambition to breathe. To live. To drive across the country on research trips. To drive, and drive on my own. To live my life the way I choose. I have ambition to be resourceful. Self-sufficient.

I persevered in the past. I will continue to persevere in what lays ahead—my return to teaching—the upheaval of getting organized to move once again. Deciding what to take, what to leave, what to store, what to give away, what to keep. I will continue to persevere in my writing also. Christ is called the Word. I want to deal in a heightened level of those kinds of words. In other words, I want to write in areas that are worthy. Is this work ambitious? It is a question I continue to ask of what I'm writing.

❦

So now I am ambitious to have my house in order. As I prepare to move from Kansas to California where I have accepted a one-year teaching appointment, I have begun the arduous task of cleaning out. I have six bookcases, which rise from the floor nearly to the ceiling. I have kept my books for years. I have a collection of important rocks. Furniture. Papers and papers, many of which I will send to the University of North Dakota library. My woolen clothes from the twenty years I lived in Minnesota. (But I've been to the Alaska Native Heritage Center in Anchorage several years in January for conferences and will need those clothes again.) Receipts for taxes. Checks I wrote long ago. Memorabilia. Correspondences. Conference programs. Drawings of my children. Their old grade cards. My old grade cards. Boxes of photographs my mother took. I also have my deceased aunt's papers. Her tax returns for the last seven years. Her photographs. How do I deal with all of this since I can't move it to California? Goodwill. Vietnam Vets of America. I have a son in Texas who said he would store some of my furniture and accumulations. My brother at the lake took my porch furniture. But a lot of what I don't need I have ambition to get rid of. I feel the intent to discard it, though I may take it back from the discard pile.

❦

After all these years, I still struggle for identity—my voice. Much of my writing is to bridge the different and disparate parts of my heritage. I still struggle for understanding of what I have to say. I struggle for place. I struggle for space to be quiet and write in this noisy and busy world. I struggle for direction in the many directions going everywhere: errands and taking care of grandchildren and other works and responsibilities of every kind. I have ambient longings. They wander into every genre and across every tribe. I work on several projects at once, being led to market (squealing) by them all. If I had to put my work process (and probably my life) into one word, it would be collage—gluing into place a mix of shapes. On the cover of my 2012 poetry book, *It Was Then*, I used a collage made by my granddaughter. Her bright pieces cut from construction paper and glued on another piece of construction paper, this one black, showed me the direction I wanted for the entry into the book. It had the primitive, folk-art feel I wanted from a book published by Mammoth Press in Lawrence, Kansas.

෯

"Optimism is true moral courage." That was what Sir Ernest Shackleton said on his 1914–16 voyage to the Antarctic when his ship, the HMS Endurance, was crushed by ice and his men were left stranded near the South Pole. It's going too far to say that writing sometimes feels like the breaking of a ship in the ice of the Antarctic sea. Think of what it must have sounded like as the sturdy boards broke apart. Can I say that ambition is true moral courage? No. But there is something about it that sounds like a ship breaking apart.

It was October 27, 1915, when the ship was crushed, leaving Shackleton and his men stranded on the ice. He traveled eight hundred miles on an open sea in a lifeboat to the island of South Georgia. Then Shackleton and two crew members traveled thirty-six hours over mountains to a whaling station. It took him nineteen months to rescue his men. What was that if not ambition?

Shackleton's story is one of abandonment and rescue—death and resurrection. Writing, for me, is a Come Back Mission that calls me constantly. Each project is a small death and resurrection, a lesser copy of God's larger plan. Often, when I start into a project, it falls apart—in other words, it dies. I put it aside and work on something else. Later, I get it out. Somewhere in the text, I find the place to begin a second time. I find the eagerness to work with it again. It is my ambition—my going around to get votes—which are the words for my writing.

Where did I get that phrase about the Come Back Mission? I was reading something, or passing something. I have myriad notes, all of them ambitiously wanting to fit somewhere in my writing. I take notes on what I see—things I pass along the road—or snippets from what I read. I'm not a careful scholar. I thrive on happenstance, though ambition takes planning and organization as well. There are voices everywhere. Warehouses of information. I have ambition to see them go somewhere. I pick up images, and whatever stays with me becomes my writing. I like whatever haunts me, whatever stays.

As I've worked over the years, I have felt chewed, crushed in the ice. I'm exaggerating. I'm over-inflating what it feels like to be squeezed by a difficult writing project, but I continue in that vein. I have an ambition to address misery, loss, discomfort. Maybe ambition is having more gumption despite circumstances. I have ambition to see the truth of what I am—a person dependent on Christ.

✧

In 1994 I went to Syria as an Arts America speaker for the United States Information Agency. After the trip, I put my notebooks/poems away in a drawer. I did send out some of the individual poems, which were published, but after several attempts of sending out the manuscript, which was rejected, I decided it was too thin. I didn't know where it was going. But in March of 2011, after the initial uprising in Syria, I took the notes from my files. I'm still working on that book, which will be a poetry collection of sorts.

I watch the horrific news, mainly on the BBC, as a Syrian government tries to crush its people. There is also a questionable (and ambitious) outside rebel force that may want to dominate the people with Islam. I want to explore these issues. I have ambition for that little book. The original title was *Necessary Departures*. Then it was *The Wind at the End of the World*. Now, as I search for the central metaphor of the manuscript, I think the title will be *Scorched Earth*. Not scorched earth as in the drought in the summer of 2012, but the scorched earth left in the wake of car bombings, firebombs, and Improvised Explosive Devices. Now the title is *The Collector of Bodies*.

I am still rewriting and adding new pieces. I should have given up in the 1990s, but I have ambition for that manuscript. It says something that has been fundamental to my life.

"Religion is the basis of everything for us," said Abdel-Aziz Salameh, one of Syria's rebel leaders struggling to topple the al-Assad regime. I would like to say the same thing. Only it would be, "Christ is the basis of everything for me." The manuscript has been significant to my struggle to understand the world in which I live. My worries over militant Islam. My worries over Islam itself. The concern over world affairs. And how can I write about my understanding of the ultimate reality without seeming bigoted? (Which I am. Christ is the only way to heaven; that is the only truth in my opinion, though I don't want to kill those who don't believe as I do.) I want to continue working with the poems in *The Collector of Bodies*. Ambition has attached itself to the book. It desires publication for the thoughts written there.

✧

I once heard Luci Shaw give a talk on our need to translate our experience into words. She mentioned the powerful impulse for affirmation that comes with publication and positive reviews. Sometimes my colleagues joked about my prolific publications, but it was what I was there to do. There is a selfishness about ambition. There is a selfishness for work. I hope so anyway, because, it seems to me, that's what writing takes.

❧

Sometimes, a book is a gift and comes quickly and easily. Ambition does not have to burn so long. I wrote the voice of Sacajawea in *Stone Heart* in two summers while following the Missouri and Columbia Rivers as I listened to the 1804–06 Lewis & Clark journals in the car. The book was published in 2004 by Overlook Press. *The Reason for Crows*, a short novel about Kateri Tekakwitha, a 17th-century Mohawk converted by the Jesuits, published in 2009 by the State University of New York, is another manuscript that came in a short period of time. I saw Kateri's figure on the front door of St. Patrick's Cathedral in New York City one year on a trip there. I did research online. The next spring, or the spring thereafter, on my way to the New England Young Writer's Conference in Middlebury, Vermont, I stopped at the ghosting or outline of Kateri's village in upstate New York near Fonda on Interstate 90. Her first-person voice, as well as the Jesuits' voices, were there, ready to fill the pages. But these books are the exception.

Mostly, a manuscript is a long effort. Often manuscripts are written together. I work on one, one day, and another, the next. I try to keep working, somewhere above discouragement. I try to keep in mind the suffering and arduous journeys of others. Who hasn't heard stories of authors sending out their manuscripts forty times before a publisher accepted it? Who hasn't heard stories of the old masters in their freezing garrets in Russia or wherever, writing their stories with scarves around their necks, gloves on their hands, trying to live on bread and tea heated on their samovars? Who doesn't know about the Old Testament prophets, reviled by the kings they prophesied against in their writings? Or the New Testament apostles, writing while on the run, leaving behind a few papers before they were martyred?

❧

Ambition takes me places, sometimes on wild rides, for example, when I move to California, where a university has invited me to teach for a year.

93

The mover says he'll be there early, but it is 10:00 a.m. before he arrives with his nephew, a veteran with "issues." Together they load the truck with what I am taking to California from my house in Kansas. The next stop is my cabin on the Lake of the Ozarks in Missouri, which has not sold, but I am emptying it anyway. Then we will drive to Texas to leave some furniture with my son and daughter-in-law. Then to Monrovia near Los Angeles.

I've hardly left my house in Kansas when the driver calls. The truck was smoking and he had to return to the shop. I think of my file boxes. My new printer cartridge, new reams of paper, my clothes, luggage, furniture, books. All my work is in that truck—my writing projects-in-progress with pages of handwritten notes and the course syllabi, which I have just completed.

While they were loading, the nephew informed me he had seizures. "Is it legal to drive with seizures?" I asked, but he said he had a license. I prayed for the nephew before they left—Heal him, God. Now I pray again—Give us a safe trip to California despite a driver with seizures and a flaming truck with all my work that cannot be recreated. Lord of risk. Lord of the cross-roads. Lord of ambition, have mercy.

I drive on to the lake in Missouri. I eat at a Mexican restaurant on the way, where they have pictures of cock fights decoupaged onto the table. There are other Mexican scenes of adobe houses and girls twirling in yellow skirts.

In a little town near the lake, I have the oil changed in my car, and the insurance on the cabin adjusted to quarters in case it sells. I pay the electric bill and give them my change of address.

When I arrive at my cabin, I sort through the boxes I had packed and wait until the movers finally arrive at nine o'clock that night. Fluid had been leaking onto the brakes, causing the smoke. The leak has to be repaired and the brakes cleaned. I go to my brother's house for the night and leave them to load the truck.

The next morning, at eight thirty, I drive to the cabin. They are still asleep. I knock on the door. They'd fished in the dark after they loaded, catching the large carp that lives under my dock, and then letting it go. I notice the fishing poles in their truck.

It is one of the hottest summers on record. Already we are sweating. Do they want to follow me? We look at the map. See—the short cut from Big Cabin, Oklahoma, to Sherman, Texas. They don't need to take Interstate 44 all the way to Oklahoma City, then south Interstate 35 to Texas. But no, they have a GPS. They don't need to follow. I watch the loaded truck climb the steep drive from my cabin. Then I sweep the floors, thank God for the place where I have come for several years to write, and lock the door. I leave for the eight-hour trip from the lake to my son's house in Texas.

It is 109° when I pass through Eufala, Oklahoma. The fields are full of dead grass. The trees have turned brown in the drought. The whole earth feels like it could go up in flames any minute. Naked I came into this world. Naked I may leave. Mid-afternoon, there are clouds in the sky. But nothing more than a few hits of rain—a splatter or two—pungent with the heavy smell of dust. I have the thought—there must be a country church nearby praying for rain.

When I arrive in Texas at evening, I call the driver. They are still in Oklahoma. They missed the turn at Big Cabin. Once again, they arrive about 9:00 p.m. After unloading some of the furniture, they are going to drive on. It is a Thursday night. They will be in California Friday night or Saturday morning at the latest. With the two of them, they can drive straight through. But I can't get there until Saturday night. It will take me two days to drive. I have the house key. I know where the furniture goes. Can I draw them a floor plan, they ask. Give them the key? I can, and do.

We look at the map again. I show them how to continue west on US 82, then US 287 through Wichita Falls to Amarillo where they will connect with Interstate 40 to California. They drive off in the dark.

I take a shower and go to bed at my son and daughter-in-law's house. I cannot sleep. I get up. There is a full moon as I drive with 169,000 miles on my car. God, is there even one moment I do not need your help? I look for the taillights of the mover's truck on the dark road ahead, but do not see them.

Around 3:00 a.m., I stop at a rest area and sleep a few hours. I should have stayed at my son's house. Eventually, I would have gone to sleep. At 6:00 a.m., driving through Memphis, Texas, with four buildings along the highway, I am stopped by Officer Jolly for doing sixty-one miles per hour through a forty-mile-an-hour zone. The fine is $183. I have two weeks to mail it in.

The next day, I call the movers and tell them I am on my way and will catch up with them. But they are back in Oklahoma. What? They had to stop in Oklahoma, they say. What does that mean? Why are they in Oklahoma where they should not be? They missed the turn, they say. What turn? It is a straight shot through Texas. Why had they turned north into Oklahoma? Where was their ambition to get to California?

Because the movers are still behind me, I can spend time in Tucumcari, New Mexico. I take exit 335 at the Tucumcari Convention Center, as if there would ever be a convention in Tucumcari. But years ago when I attended the Grace and Glory Bible Church, I came to a church camp of sorts, an adult church camp, where others of the same beliefs gathered for a week of revival.

The first stop light in Tucumcari turns red. That will take up two minutes. I drive along old Route 66 that runs through Tucumcari, past decaying motels and closed restaurants. I pass scrub brush in empty lots. Boarded-up buildings with faded signs. Rusting cars and trucks at filling stations no longer in operation. I find a Walmart and Dickinson's Implement Company with a lot full of large galvanized tanks. A few other stores are labeled "Ranch Supplies." What to do for the morning?—Find the library. Get online. Have lunch at Del's. Kill as much time as possible. After I fill the car with gasoline, there's nothing else to do. I get on I-40 west, and pass four patrol cars, one in the median, one stopped behind a car, two roaming the east and west lanes. I should have warned the movers.

When I call them again, I ask how they are doing. Not good. A highway patrol car stopped them at Tucumcari to inspect their papers. There is a mandatory ten-hour rest for long-distance drivers. The officer looked at their logbook. There is no sleep rack in the truck. They had to stop. The officer escorted them to a motel in Tucumcari.

In the afternoon, I stop at a large rest area east of Albuquerque. There is shade in one of the far corners—and a breeze, probably from the passing trucks. I close my eyes for a while before I drive across the rest of New Mexico into Arizona.

That night, I sleep at another rest area, this one just east of Flagstaff. The next morning, I stop at the Starbucks in Flagstaff and spend several hours online again. One of the deans at the college where I'm headed is asking the faculty for a list of publications—he needs a brag list for funders—another slot for my ambition. Then I look at the map to find a place to meet. I call the movers again. We will meet at the exit for Williams. I spend more time in Arizona waiting for them.

Then, there they come down the highway. We greet. They will follow me to LA and not get lost again. But they are slow. I get too far ahead of them, and they are gone again. I wait at another rest area. I call them again.

We meet up again in Needles, California. They want to rest. The truck is slow in the heat. One mountain pass was marked seven thousand feet. They'll get an early start Sunday morning.

I stop at a rest area in the desert of California on I-40 east of Barstow, and lay my head on a pillow for a moment. A two-day trip has turned into four. My car is old. It is 105°. How will the movers find my duplex on their own with a GPS that took them north when they should have gone west?

I am at a low point. I am lost in the desert. But Christ had gone before me, the root out of my dry ground. The spark that holds me. I can drive on.

I arrive in Monrovia in early evening. I enter the empty duplex. Take the sleeping bag, the mat, the bedding and pillow from the back of my car. Place them on the floor. I sleep.

The movers arrive in mid-morning on Sunday. They unload. I write them a check. We pray at the table. We say good-bye.

Monday, I get a new phone number.

Tuesday morning, I open my front door at 7:00 a.m. to find the mover standing there. He had to take the nephew to the Veteran's Administration hospital in Los Angeles for his seizures, which he says the hospital calls episodes. When the doctor induced a seizure, the scan did not show brain waves coming from the usual place that seizures come from. Maybe it was the load of memories the nephew carried from his deployment to Afghanistan. The mover wants me to take him to a bank where he can cash the check I gave him so he can have some money.

We get on the 210 in morning traffic. We arrive at the bank in Pasadena. It's still an hour before it opens. We go to breakfast at Russell's and he tells me of his childhood, and the troubles he's been in, including jail, and how he decided he had to get straightened out.

God, bless the people with lives that are one long drive to California after another, yet they find the ambition to drive on.

I ask the mover again, is he a Christian? It's the question I asked before I hired him. The answer is still yes. Oh God of mercy—have mercy on these men who brought their fishing poles in the truck—the mover and his nephew who, he tells me, only came because he wanted to fish in the ocean.

⤙⤚

As I struggle with different manuscripts, I hope ambition does not leave me. I have the voices of ten biblical women in *Uprising of Goats*. I have a novel on Alzheimer's called *No Word for the Sea* in which forgetfulness of God is a contemporary spiritual Alzheimer's. It was published in 2013 by Just Fiction! Edition, Av Omni Scriptum, Saarbruken, Germany. I have a novel about the murder of ten people in Wichita, Kansas, called, *The Man Who Set Himself Up as God*, now titled *One of Us*. BTK (bind, torture, kill), is the name Denis Rader gave himself. He was president of the congregation of the church he attended for years while committing his murders. There are several books about Rader, but I want to look at the devastation the congregation faced after he was arrested. How does a minister deal with a murderer in his own congregation? What is the nature of evil? How do we face it? What is our resilience to it? Can a Christian commit murder and remain a Christian? What is the definition of a Christian? The more I write, the more questions I uncover.

Is there an unselfish ambition? A tamed ambition? A sanctified ambition? I would like to think so, though it seems doubtful. Nonetheless— thank you, ambition, for being in my life. You are there to motivate. Forgive my selfishness, Lord and family. Recently I was working on a piece and took off a weekend to drive to Texas to be with my son's family. My daughter-in-law asked me to stay longer. My son had a busy week and she would be alone with the four-year-old. But I could not. I was burning to get back to my house in Kansas, nine hours away, to continue work on my project— actually projects. I have lived alone for many years. The noise of cartoons on television bothers me. I want my space. I want privacy. There's the dicey edge of ambition. I couldn't set my ambition aside. I wanted my life.

Ambition is the fuel that holds the many opposing fragments of my life together. Ambition is a buffer zone. A war zone. All the contradictions that are within me. I have had talented students who didn't seem to be ambitious for their work. I wanted to tell them, get going. Talent isn't enough. I did tell them to send out their work. I also wanted to ask myself, why am I driven to achieve?

For a little while you may have to suffer various trials, I read in 1 Peter 1:6.

"Come to that living stone, rejected by men, but in God's sight chosen and precious," I find in 1 Peter 2:4. Somehow there is peace in the middle of the struggle. Somehow, I know where I'm going even though the unknown lies ahead. It is never easy. That is one of the lines I added to the dialogue of my independent film when I was in the process of filming.

᭜

I think the ultimate creative ambition I faced was in the making of an independent film in 2009–10, titled *The Dome of Heaven*. In the 1980s, I worked for the State Arts Council of Oklahoma as Artist in Residence. I wrote a novel, *Flutie*, about a mixed-blood girl who wanted to go to college despite the poverty of her family and her low self-esteem. Flutie was part myself and part of the many students I saw on the back rows of classrooms. I included the land in the film. The dome of heaven is the western Oklahoma sky and the heavy sun that travels there. I cannot drive through western Oklahoma—across the Salt Plains, through the Glass Mountains, past the green fields and red ponds—without recognizing the impact of the land. In 1998, the year the novel was published by Moyer Bell, I received a Sundance Institute's Native Lab Fellowship, where I turned *Flutie* into the script. I kept the script in my files for twelve years, remembering it now and then, filling out a few grants to make a film, but nothing ever happened. Still, ambition to make the film stayed with me.

I retired from teaching at Macalester College and moved to Kansas to help with three grandchildren and three aging relatives. I taught two semesters at Kenyon College and banked most of the money. When one of my old relatives died, I had an inheritance. Could I use the money to make a film? I asked my brother.

Do it, he said, before you're too old to do it. I also told him that if I had been the one on the death bed, I would have said, I wish I had made that film. I begin without enough money to finish the film, but other people, mainly in Oklahoma, give money to the project. We filmed for two weeks, once in December 2009, and once in April 2010, and then closed it down. I was not going into debt. We edited what we had, and the film was made.

I have a note on the process of independent filmmaking on my website, http://www.dianeglancy.com, under Film. It begins, "Dreams are dangerous." They uncover your bones. Each day there was a disaster of one sort or another to muddle through. The first day of shooting in December, I woke at 4:00 a.m. to hear sleet against the window. We had a thirty-mile drive on a narrow road to Taloga to film the courtroom scene. The last night of shooting in April, there was a deluge. Water ran across the floor of the Cedar Shack among the wires for our equipment. But the film was made, and I've taken it to film festivals and on a few college circuits.

I am in love with ambition. I am burdened with ambition. I ask for ambition to come and bother me. I ask for ambition to leave. Ambition is a statement that defines me. I am unsettled by ambition. I am settled by ambition. I am torn with ambition. I am certain about ambition. Ambition is a blessing. Ambition is a curse. It is the best of times. It is the worst. Ambition reveals my weakness. Ambition is my strength. I wish I was ambitious for patience. For peace and kindness. For gentleness and quietness. I live alone, so quietness is easier. I wish ambition was a friend of meekness. As I've already said, I need ambition to keep going. I want to move ambition from my plate. Ambition weighs too much to move. It sits in my workroom like a walrus. Its tusks are pure ivory. Or is that the elephant? Maybe walrus tusks are only bone. May I have the ambition to look it up.

8

Why Run When You Can Fly?

Gina Ochsner

How terrible it will be for you who add more houses to your houses and more fields to your fields until there is no room left for other people. Then you are left alone in the land.

ISAIAH 5:8 NCV

WHEN I WAS ELEVEN years old, I had two ambitions: to be more like the elite marathon runner Grete Waitz and to be more like the stunt motorcyclist Evel Knievel. Running shoes being more readily available than Harleys, I ran. Past the fields of kale and strawberries, past the ominous orchards where darkness brewed between trunks and canopies of tight foliage. Except for the few times I got lost in those orchards, the running struck me as mundane. Why do runners punish themselves like this? I wondered as I trudged along. The track coach suggested that I memorize motivational platitudes to keep my inner morale from flagging. *When the going gets tough, the tough get going. No pain, no gain.* My favorite: "Motivation is when dreams roll up their sleeves and get to work." While I never stopped admiring the determination of Grete who ran without sweating, who moved like a machine, tireless and steady, winning nine New York City Marathons, it was Craig "Evel" Knievel whose poster graced the back of my brother's bedroom door; it was Evel Knievel who I really wanted to be. Evel

Knievel would never plod along broken asphalt at these pedestrian speeds; Evel Knieval would never be so ordinary as to run when he could fly.

Equal parts showman and daredevil, Knievel envisioned feats few had imagined. That took inspiration. His defied gravity with the heaviest of bikes. That took courage. If he successfully jumped ten cars, then the next jump he'd try to clear eleven. If eleven, then twelve. And so on and so forth until he graduated to jumping buses. Then buses while first clearing walls of fire. In 1975 he attempted a thirteen-bus jump at Wembley Stadium in London. He failed the jump but that didn't keep him down. Six months later at Kings Island amusement park in Ohio he attempted and successfully completed a fourteen-bus jump. He made a twenty-foot hop over a box of live rattlers. He attempted to jump the three-quarter-mile-wide Snake River Canyon near Twin Falls, Idaho, on his Skycycle X-2, fitted with a small rocket. This required motivation, ambition even, of a peculiar sort and a parachute that readily deployed. In the course of his long and illustrious career, he broke 433 bones, easily landing him in the *Guinness Book of World Records* for the most bones broken.* In an interview, Knievel recounted how every bone in his body had been broken, some more than once. Describing himself as "nothing but scar tissue and surgical steel," the trauma he sustained during his many stunts necessitated many artificial replacements, and these, he said, had all been broken, too. No doubt he'd been asked many times: why keep jumping? The daredevil's unfailing answer: because he'd given his word. When pressed by reporters he'd give a trademark grin and say, "I am an explorer."

Uncomfortable in the presence of paradox, the notion that an idea, a concept like love, beauty, or say, ambition, can maintain multiple definitions, each of them true, puzzles me. Even worse, the word represents an abstraction. I can't even touch it, taste it, or smell it. Trying to define this abstraction is like trying to put together a three-dimensional puzzle, the pieces of which have no firm boundaries. I am reminded of my limited vocabulary, my inability to pin the precise word to a thing and so peg it, place it. It occurs to me I may not be alone in my frustration. Or maybe I'm just confused. Assuming a myriad of shapes and functions, when used as a noun the word seems simple enough. It's a thing. And it's a thing you either have or you

---

* Knieval often claimed that he had broken only 35 bones.

don't. *Merriam-Webster* defines ambition as an ardent desire for rank, fame, or power. The word takes its origins from the Latin *ambire* which means literally the act of soliciting for votes. In modern usage it seems to mean anything from inordinate desire to motivation to gumption, to get-up-and-go. The broad range of descriptions assigned to the word suggests that it gathers meaning and weight depending upon context and degree. Perhaps this is why ambition is defined by some as a driving passion to accomplish or acquire something. Hall of Fame basketball player Bill Bradley described ambition as "the path to success. Persistence is the vehicle you arrive in," while others define it as doing the best you have with what God has given you. OK. So, maybe ambition is more than a mere *thing*. Maybe it's action or an attitude that shapes action.

Used as an adjective, the word can be a compliment or used in a complimentary fashion, but more often than not pejorative. "That's an ambitious project," means you haven't got a snowball's chance in hell. "He's ambitious," means he's a jackass. "She's set her sights on more ambitious things," means she's a grasping climber: watch out. "*That's* ambitious," means it's way out of your league. Then there are the adjective-noun combos. Selfish ambition. Blind ambition. Stupid ambition. A word so slippery it needs these adjectives to cut it down to size.

I've heard of ambition spoken of in reverential tones. I've heard the word uttered as if it were one of the deadliest of sins, certainly not a character trait one wants to acquire.

Given the broad range of value and interpretation assigned to the word and because of the varied contexts it is used, little wonder, then, that the word evokes confusion.

⟜⟞

My brother and I grew up in a culture of highly motivated individuals. What is your goal today? What are your three-month, six-month, and one-year goals? were frequently asked questions in my family. If we made the mistake of saying "I don't know," someone might whip out a thermometer. The absence of goals clearly could mean only one thing: you were sick. At family gatherings there was much talk about pulling oneself up by the bootstraps. The work ethic went something like this: *work hard. If things look bad, work harder. If that doesn't help, work smarter.* Motivation's twin sister was ambition; they could convincingly swap places.

❧

Dr. Seuss provides an illustration of ambition in the tale *Yurtle the Turtle*. Yurtle, an important turtle in his pond, doesn't like the limited view the muddy pond affords. Yurtle orders some underlings to climb upon each other's backs and form a miniature turtle tower. Yurtle then climbs to the top of the turtle stack. The view is nice and Yurtle commends himself on his achievement: he is now king of all he can see, in this case the pond. Then an idea: a gain in altitude would give him a larger, better view. More underlings are ordered to climb the turtle stack, and Yurtle sits atop them, king of all he sees. What he sees is nice: a field, some trees. Then an idea: there must be more. More underlings climb the turtle tower. Yurtle is sitting high and lofty, but it's not long before he gets an idea. His underlings can hardly maintain their fragile balance: they've been burdened by Yurtle's "vision" for some time now. But Yurtle is not troubled by their shaking knees and buckling legs. He orders more turtles to climb the stack. We suppose this would go on forever, the turtle pile increasing turtle by turtle. But then, the unthinkable. Someone sneezes. The turtle tower wobbles. Unceremoniously and in a most undignified manner, Yurtle tumbles to the mud. Wanting for the sake of wanting at the expense of others, and a sneeze was Yurtle's undoing.

What business has a turtle with the weighty matter at hand? To answer that, I must travel through time and place to the high north, 1800s. For reasons I find baffling and in no way can explain, I became fascinated by the many polar expeditions and the brave undertakings of explorers in search first of the Northwest Passage and then later the precise locations of the North and South Poles. I poured over the field reports, letters, sketches, admiralty reports, and journal entries of Fridtjof Nansen and Peary, Scott, and others who wrote of icebergs and their magnificent cathedral beauty, the mineral greens of melting ice water on larger pans of ice, the music of ice melt, the growl of a glacier in motion. They wrote of the dance of lights in the sky over the ice, the ferocity of a wind that unthreads nuts on bolts. We are lucky that theirs was a day of journal keeping and letter writing. Because in these accounts penned in their own hand, crafted in their own voices, we perceive through the gaps and spaces of the prose glimpses of the men.

In his journals we read of a Robert Peary who is as interested in photographing tiny sprigs of saxifrage as he is in capturing on film enormous hummocks of ice. His journals reflect his utter astonishment at finding that the cliffs of Western Greenland were not, in fact, green, but red. He marveled at the live volcanoes ringed in snow and the red poppies blooming in ice crags. His intrepid wife, a formidable trail blazer by his accounts, often accompanied him. On the days when he convinced her to stay at camp while he foraged for food and specimen, his entries reflect a hint of relief.

He wasn't the first to explore West Greenland or map the numerous channels, inlets, and bays between eastern Canada and Greenland. Still, he attained notoriety when he was the first (or claimed to be the first) to reach the North Pole in 1909. In defense of his pursuits he writes:

> To those who, in the absence of a dollar-for-dollar return for every effort, ask "Of what earthly use is Arctic exploration?" I might answer: "What is the use of yacht race, of athletic contests, of trials of engines, and war-ships, of any of the innumerable tests that have, since the world was young, been man's only means of determining the superiority of one man, or one machine, or one method, or one nation, over another?"

No doubt Roald Amundsen had these same thoughts in mind when he raced against Robert Scott for the South Pole. Keenly aware of the bitter conflict between Frederick Cook and Peary and their competing claims of having been the first to attain the pole, when he attained the South Pole in December of 1911, Amundsen made it a point to ring the pole with a series of Norwegian flags. In a cairn he left a stash of food and a congratulatory note for Scott who would not reach the Pole for another five weeks. Scott would not leave Antarctica alive and, what we know of him, too, becomes apparent in his last letters penned "to his widow." His tone remains stalwart, brave. This was the age of exploration and the high North and South were the last frontiers.

Fifty some odd years prior to Peary's adventures, Sir John Franklin captured the public stage. In 1843, Franklin strode onto the ice in his naval high hat and braided uniform. Arguably the largest and most expensive Arctic expedition ever mounted, he'd been supplied with the best navigational equipment of the day, a ship with a steel-reinforced keel, three years worth of provisions, which, among other things, included 1,000 pounds of mustard, 10,088 pounds of raisins, and 100 Bibles. Within the year he was dead, his crew lost and scattered.

What Franklin had gone after and lost his life for was an open Northwest trading route. The quest didn't make much sense, even in 1843. The British Admiralty had received reports as early as 1834 from William Parry and James Clark Ross, who scouted the Boothia Peninsula where he pinpointed determined magnetic north. They had been searching for an open Northwest Passage without luck. Their maps and charts led the Admiralty to believe that even if such a route could be traversed, it would yield little mercantile value. Their quest was more a matter of patriotism and pride, and to a lesser extent scientific curiosity. The English had opened the door to the High North but had not really crossed the threshold. They did not want the French and Russians to beat them to it. In the manner and spirit of the 1960s space race, the British, French, and Russians were eager to be the first to open the passage. And so, after the first three candidates declined the commission, the Admiralty settled on Franklin who seemed eager for the job. Some historians have suggested that it was an ambitious undertaking and taken for the sake of ambition only. Whose ambition it is hard to say, but the loss of Franklin and his crew spurred a renewed interest in the beautiful and terrible High North.

In the winter of 1849 the Admiralty offered a £20,000 reward to any ship that located and aided Franklin. Between 1848 and 1853 no less than thirty expeditions and forty ships were launched in the search for Franklin and his men. All to no avail.

Dissatisfied by the lack of concrete information and certain that these expeditions had been dispatched too far north and east of where her husband was last sighted, and having received psychic tips from the ghost of a girl who had died of consumption, Lady Franklin financed and organized her own expedition. At this point, the Admiralty could offer little financial help: the Crimean War diverted their attention to more pressing matters. In 1857, eleven years after the disappearance of Franklin and his men, Lady Franklin again organized a private expedition, commanded by Francis Leopold McClintock. On King William Island, McClintock and his men found forks and spoons bearing the crests of Franklin and some of his officers. Likewise, as they made their way south along the shore line, following the trail of the Franklin expedition, they found skeletal remains as well as more impedimenta: a stone jug, a rifle case, a sextant bearing the name of a seaman from Franklin's expedition. Nonessentials and essentials alike were strewn along the coastline, evidence of a terrible march in which the ranks thinned as one by one the men succumbed to scurvy and starvation. Though McClintock could not account for the exact whereabouts of all the men numbered in Franklin's party, he had seen enough to make an educated guess.

No one was more interested in Franklin and the fate of his lost crew than thirty-eight-year-old Charles Hall. A moderately successful Cincinnati businessman, Hall ran a newspaper and engraving shop. He scuttled both to finance an Arctic expedition, the purpose of which was to determine definitively what had happened to Franklin and to ascertain whether or not there were survivors. Though he wrote many letters to prominent politicians, lobbying hard for his cause, few made contributions. He ended up providing most of his own support. His wife wrote him a check for $27.

By this time, McClintock's discoveries had been made public. Undeterred, Hall continued his preparations. In Hall's opinion, too many questions remained unanswered. And though he had scant formal education, no experience in exploration or knowledge of the Arctic other than what he gleaned from newspapers, Hall possessed a singular and preternatural confidence. Moreover, Hall felt he'd been commissioned; he believed that he heard a voice calling him to look for Franklin, and that voice was none other than God's.

Unfamiliar with the paradoxical nature of ice—its solidity and fluidity, the difference between floe ice and solid pack—untrained in navigation, unschooled in the eccentricities of navigating in an area where the magnetism would confound an experienced navigator, Hall seemed an improbable explorer. What he lacked in knowledge he made up for with enthusiasm. He taught himself navigation from a textbook; cold weather survival by pitching a tent in the hills behind the Cincinnati Observatory. He spent several nights in the cool autumn in an attempt to simulate an Arctic experience and inure himself to the rigors of that climate. As it turns out, the only hardship he encountered during this tent training was the unexpected arrival of two drunken Irishmen. Looking for whiskey and learning that Hall had none, they routed him from his tent. Hall, nearly naked, fled the hills for his home.

Finally, Hall managed to collect enough money to outfit a ship, obtain provisions, a crew. Few expected him to survive. When he did, it was considered something of a miracle. Even odder was his determination to return to the High North as soon as possible. His rationale confounded even his staunchest supporters. He had not located any new evidence suggesting that any of Franklin's men might still be alive. He had not conducted any real research nor had he discovered or navigated new territory. And yet, in his characteristic manner, Hall remained convinced that he was conducting vital and essential work. In fact, upon returning from his first expedition, he wrote, "It seemed to me as if I had been called." All told, Hall would launch three expeditions to the High North.

Equal parts charming and gruff, Hall had a way of making friends and losing them. What we know of his friendships and what we know of him, we have Hall to thank. A prolific writer, he recorded his every action and thought, enthusiastically underscoring his words with lines and exclamation points.

He'd travel to a place so cold, he'd have to cut out chunks of ink and boil them to a putty before he could write. His notes often assumed epic tones of grandeur some might consider pathological. "GOD," he wrote, "BE THANKED, I AM SAVED!" Hall wrote after a near miss with his pistol. He had stooped to examine quartz embedded in a rock, when the gun fell from his holster and discharged. The sound and the powder burns on his face momentarily convinced him that he had been shot. Upon discovering his full deliverance from harm, he immediately journalled: "I have just escaped with my life. PROVIDENTIALLY ESCAPED! No other arm but the Almighty's could have saved me. . . ." One gets the sense that this miracle served only to reinforce Hall's fervor for his new vocation as a self-made explorer. Clearly God was on his side. He would need all the help he could get.

In spite of his verbosity, exuberance, and cliché, biographer Chauncy Loomis notes that "the man himself would occasionally emerge, looking out at the world with a diffidence that only partly concealed his driving energy and ambition." He would embark on three expeditions in the course of ten years. During that time his wife would bear him two children with whom he would spend a total of two months. For all his enthusiasm, piety, and drive, Hall would never become the famous explorer he had hoped to be. And to be fair, perhaps Hall wasn't interested in fame. Perhaps his travels to the High North represented for him the realization of a lifelong dream to do something different, unusual. To escape in an unusual manner. During his third expedition, Hall died of arsenic poisoning. His body was buried in a place so far north a needle on a compass points southwest.

Hall's story, his life, verges on the extreme, the absurd. His ambition makes little sense. But I don't have to read books about explorers to find weird and tragic ambition. I could examine myself, my insistent pursuit of publication. I could turn on the TV. And there I am confronted, confounded by obsession with beauty, youth, perfection. I am ashamed to admit that from time to time, for the sheer OMG factor, I watch *Toddlers and Tiaras*. Where else can I view motherly ambition served up so raw and naked?

9

Toward Humility

Bret Lott

5

ONCE IT'S OVER, YOU write it all down in second person so that it doesn't sound like you who's complaining. So it doesn't sound like a complaint.

Because you have been blessed.

You have been blessed.

You have been blessed.

And still you know nothing, and still it all sounds like a complaint.

⊖

4

You are on a Learjet.

It's very nice: plush leather seats for which leg room isn't even a matter, the jet seating only six; burled wood cabinets holding beer and sodas; burled wood drawers hiding bags of chips, boxes of cookies, cans of nuts; copies of three of today's newspapers; a stereo system loaded with CDs.

Your younger son, age thirteen, is with you, invited along with the rest of your family by the publicist for the bookstore chain whose jet this is. When you and your wife and two sons pulled up to the private end of the airport in the town where you live, there on the tarmac had sat a Learjet out of which came first the publicist, a young and pretty woman in a beige business suit, followed by the pilots, who introduced themselves with just their first names—Hal and John—and shook hands with each member of your family.

"You're all welcome to come along," the publicist had said, and you'd seen she meant it. But it was an invitation made on the spot, nothing you had planned for. And since your older son, fifteen, has a basketball tournament, and your wife has to drive, it is left to your younger son to come along.

Your younger son, the one who has set his heart and mind and soul upon being a pilot. The one whose room is plastered with posters of jets. The one who has memorized his copy of *Jane's Military Aircraft*.

"I guess we can get you a toothbrush," you'd said to him, and here had come a smile you knew was the real thing, his eyebrows up, mouth open, deep breaths in and out, in his eyes a joyful disbelief at this good fortune. All in a smile.

Now here you are, above clouds. In a Learjet, your son in the jump-seat—leather, too—behind the cockpit, talking to Hal and John, handing them cans of Diet Coke, the publicist talking to you about who else has ridden in the corporate jet. Tom Wolfe, she tells you. Patricia Cornwell. Jimmy Carter. And a writer who was so arrogant she won't tell you his name.

This is nowhere you'd ever thought you might be. Sure, you may have hoped a book you wrote might someday become a bestseller, but it wasn't a serious hope. More like hoping to win the lottery. A pretty thought, but not a whole lot you could do about it, other than write the best you knew how.

But getting on a list wasn't why you wrote, and here, at 37,000 feet and doing 627 miles an hour over a landscape so far below you, you see, really, nothing, there is in you a kind of guilt, a sense somehow you are doing something you shouldn't be doing.

Riding in a Learjet to go to a bookstore—four of them in two days—to sign copies of your book.

Your book: published eight years before, out of print for the last two. A book four books ago, one you'd thought dead and gone, the few copies left from the one and only hardcover print run available in remainder bins at book warehouses here and there around the country.

A book about your family based on the life of your grandmother who raised six children, all of whom were born in a log cabin your grandfather built, the last of those six a Down Syndrome baby, a daughter born in 1943 and for whom little hope of living was held out by the doctors of the time. It is about your grandmother and the love she had for that baby, her desire to see her live, and her own desire to fix things for her daughter as best she could if even at the cost of her other children and, perhaps, her husband.

A book recently anointed by a celebrity talk show host. Not a celebrity, but an icon. Not an icon, but a Force. A person so powerful and influential that simply by announcing the name of your book a month ago, it has been born again.

Bigger than you had ever imagined it might become. Bigger than you had ever allowed yourself even to dream. Even bigger than that. And bigger.

Guilt, because it seems you're some kind of impostor. Even though it is based on your family, you had to reread the novel for the first time since you last went through it, maybe nine years ago, when it was in galleys, you, sick of it by that time to the point where, like all the other books you have published—there are eight in all—you don't read them again. But this one you had to reread so that you could know who these characters were, know the intricate details of their lives so that if someone on the television show were to ask a question of an obscure moment in the whole of it all, you would have seemed to them and to the nation—Who would be watching? How many people? As many as have bought the book? And more, of course—to be on close terms with the book, with its people, its social context and historical and spiritual significance.

You wrote it ten years ago.

And yesterday you were on this talk show host's program.

Tom Wolfe, you think. Jimmy Carter, and you realize you are dressed entirely wrong, in your dull green sweater and khaki pants, old leather shoes. Maybe you should have worn a sport coat. Maybe a tie. Definitely better shoes.

You can see the soles of your son's skateboard shoes, worn nearly through at the balls of his feet, him on his knees and as far into the cockpit as he can get. He's got on a pair of cargo shorts, the right rear pocket torn, and a green T-shirt. He'd been lucky enough to wear a polar fleece jacket to the airport this February morning in the sunny South.

This is all wrong.

The publicist continues on about who has ridden in the corporate jet, and you nod, wondering, How did I get here?

All you know is that you wrote this book and received a phone call the first week in January, a call that came on a very bad day for you, a call that found you out a thousand miles from your home, where you were teaching others how they might learn to write. A job in addition to the daily teaching job you have so that you might make ends meet, and so that your wife wouldn't have to work as many hours as she has in the past.

The Force found you there, on a very bad day, and gave you unbelievable news. And now your book is on the lists.

You think about that day. About how very bad it was, how empty, and hollow, and how even the news that was the biggest news of your life was made small by what happened.

And now the plane begins its initial descent into the metropolis, and your son returns to the seat beside you, still with that incredulous smile, though you have been airborne nearly an hour. Hal and John happily announce you'll be landing in moments, the landscape below hurrying into view—trees, highways, cars, homes. Nothing different from the view out any airplane window you have looked before, but different all the way around.

Everything is different.

The jet settles effortlessly to the ground, taxies to the private end of an airport you've flown into before, the public terminal out your window but far, far away, and you see, there on the tarmac as the jet eases to a stop, a Mercedes limousine.

You look at your shoes, and at your son's. His cargo shorts. This sweater you have on.

"When we were here with Jimmy Carter, the lines were all the way out the store and halfway around the building," the publicist says. "This is going to be fun," she says, and smiles, stands, heads out the door past smiling, nodding Hal and John.

Then John asks, "What would you guys like for dinner?"

You and your son look at each other—he's still smiling, still smiling—and then you look to John, shrug, smile. "Subs?" you say, as if the request might be too much to manage.

"No problem," John says, and both he and Hal nod again.

Here is the store: brick, tall, a presence. A single store in a huge bookstore chain, every store complete with a coffee bar and bakery, a gift shop with coffee mugs and T-shirts and calendars.

And books.

You climb out of the limousine before the chauffeur can get around to open your door, because you don't want to make him feel like you're the kind of person who will wait for a door to be opened. Then you and your son, the publicist in the lead, make your way for the front doors.

Inside is a huge poster in a stand, the poster two feet by four feet, advertising your being at this store for a signing. In the center of the poster is your picture, formidable and serious, it seems to you. Too serious. This isn't you, you think. That person staring pensively off the photographer's left shoulder is somebody posing as an author, you think.

There are a few people in the store, and you wonder if the line will form a little later on once the signing gets underway, and you are ushered by a smiling store manager in a red apron to the signing area.

It's in the middle of the store, and is a table stacked with copies of the anointed book, and with reprints of the earlier three books, and of the four that have come out since the anointed one first appeared all those years ago. Your books, you see, are piled everywhere. Books, and books.

"Look at this!" the manager exclaims, and points like a game show hostess to a rack of paperback books beside you, the Bestseller rack. "You're the number one book," the manager says, and you see the rows of your book, beneath them a placard with #1 printed on it.

You look at your son to see if he's as impressed as you are beginning to be.

He smiles at you, nods at the books, his eyebrows up.

He's impressed.

You take your seat behind the table laden with your books and see between the stacks that there is a kind of runway that extends out from the front of your table to the other end of the store, a long and empty runway paved with gray-blue carpet. Big, and wide, and empty. "We'll get you some coffee and cookies, if that's all right," the publicist says to you, then, to your son, "Hot chocolate sound good?" and your son says, "Yes ma'am," and, "Thank you."

You are here. The signing has begun.

But there are no customers.

You wait, while the manager announces over the in-store speakers your presence, fresh from yesterday's appearance on national TV. This drives a couple of people to the runway, and they walk down the long corridor of gray-blue carpet toward you. It seems it takes a long time for them to make it to you, longer even than the flight up here from your hometown, and you smile at these people coming at you: a young man, tall and lanky; a woman your age with glasses and short brown hair.

They are smiling at you.

You know them. Students of yours from the program where you teach a thousand miles from home. They are students of yours, friends, writers. Both of them.

You stand, hug them both, introduce them to your son, to the manager back from the announcement, and to the publicist returning now with that coffee and hot chocolate, those cookies. Then the three of you remark upon the circumstance of your meeting here: they live in the same city and have been waiting for your appearance at the store; how wonderful and strange that your book has been picked, what a blessing! When Jimmy Carter came here, the line was out the door and halfway around the building.

You talk, sip at the coffee, don't touch the cookie. There are no other customers, and the manager promises they will come, they will come. He's had phone calls all day asking when you will get here and if the lines will be too long to wait through.

You talk more, and more. Talk that dwindles to nothing, but what is not being said: where are the customers?

Now, finally, fifteen minutes into a two-hour signing, you see an older woman rounding the end of the runway. She has bright orange hair piled high and wears a tailored blue suit. She's pushing a stroller, and you imagine she is a grandmother out with her grandchild, the child's mother perhaps somewhere in the store right now, searching out children's books while Grandma takes care of the baby.

It's an expensive suit, you can tell as she moves closer, maybe thirty feet away now, and you see too the expensive leather bag she carries with her. The baby is still hidden under blankets, and you smile at the woman as she moves closer, closer, a customer heralding perhaps more customers, maybe even a line out the store and halfway around the building by the time this is all over.

Then here is the woman arriving at the other side of the table, and you see between the stacks she is even older than you believed. Heavy pancake makeup serves in a way that actually makes her wrinkles bigger, thicker; watery eyes are almost lost in heavy blue eye shadow; penciled-in eyebrows arch high on her forehead.

And you are smiling at this person, this customer, as she slowly bends to the stroller and says in the same moment, "Here's the famous writer,

Sophie, the famous writer Mommy wants you to meet," and she lifts from inside the blankets, the woman cooing all the while and making kissing sounds now, a dog.

A rat dog, a pink bow in the thin brown fur between its pointy ears.

"Sophie," the woman says to the dog, "would you mind if Mommy lets the famous writer hold you?" and her arms stretch toward you between the stacks of your books, in her hands this dog with a pink ribbon, and without thinking you reach toward her, and now you are holding Sophie.

The dog whimpers, shivers, licks its lips too quickly, tiny eyes darting again and again away from you to Mommy.

You don't know what to say, only smile, nod, and let your own eyes dart to your students, these friends, who stand with their own smiles, eyes open perhaps a little too wide, and then you glance behind you to the publicist, whose chin is a little too high and whose mouth is open, and to the manager, who stands with her arms crossed against her red apron. She's looking at the gray-blue carpet.

And here is your son. He's standing at the end of this line of people, hands behind his back, watching. He's not smiling, his mouth a straight line, and your eyes meet a moment.

He's watching.

"Sophie would love it," the woman begins, and you turn to her. She's plucked a copy of the anointed book from one of the piles, has opened it to the title page. Those watery eyes are nearly lost in the wrinkles gathering from the force of her smile. "I know Sophie would absolutely love it," she continues, "if you were to sign this copy to her."

You swallow, still smiling. "For Sophie?" you say.

The woman nods, reaches toward you for the dog, and you hand it out to her while she says, "She'll love it. She'd be so very proud."

Here is your book, open and ready to be signed.

You look at your students. Their faces are no different, still smiling. They are looking at you.

You look at the publicist, and the manager. They are both looking at you, too.

And you look to your son. He has his hands at his sides now, his mouth still that thin, straight line. But his eyes have narrowed, looking at you, scrutinizing you in a way that speaks so that only you can hear, This is what happens when you're famous?

These are the exact words you hear from his eyes, narrowed, scrutinizing.

"She would be so very proud," the woman says, and you look to her again, Sophie up to her face now, and licking her cheek, that pancake makeup.

You pull from your shirt pocket your pen.

⬦

3

Everyone is here, your living room choked with friends, maybe fifty people in all, all there to watch the show. You and your wife have laid out platters of Buffalo wings, fresh vegetables, jalapeño poppers, various cheeses and crackers and dip; there are bowls of chips, a vast array of soft drinks. Cups have been filled with store-bought ice, paper plates and napkins and utensils all spread out.

They are here for the celebration. You, on the Force's talk show, your book the feature.

Kids swirl around the house and out in the yard, their parents laughing and eating and asking what it was like to meet her, to be with her, to talk with her. Some of them tell you, too, that they have finally read your book and tell you how wonderful your book was.

You've known most of these people for years, and there are moments that come to you while these friends tell you how wonderful your book was when you want to ask them, Why didn't you read it when it came out eight years ago? But you only smile, tell them all the same thing: thank you, thank you, thank you.

You tell them, too, that the Force was incredibly intelligent, disarming, genuine, better read than you yourself are. A genuine, genuine person.

This was what she was like when you met her, when you taped the show for three hours two weeks ago, you and her book club guests—four women, each of whom wrote a letter about the effect of your book on their lives that was convincing enough to get the producers of the show to fly them in, be these book club guests—and there were moments during that whole afternoon when, seated next to her and listening to one or another of the guests, you stole a look at her and told yourself, That's her. That's her. I'm sitting next to her. Moments that startled you with the reality of this all,

moments that in the next moment you had to shut down for fear that thinking this way would render you wordless, strike you dumb with celebrity
were the conversation to turn abruptly to you.

Then the show begins. Kids still swirl, and your wife has to pull two
preschoolers from the computer in the sunroom off the living room, where
they are banging two-fisted each on the keyboard, no one other than you
and your wife seeming to notice this, everyone watching the television.
There are no empty chairs left, no space on the sofa, the carpet in front of
the TV spread with people sitting, paper plates in hand heaped with Buffalo
wings and jalapeño poppers and veggie sticks, and you have no choice but
to stand in the back of the room, watching.

Here is what you were warned of: this episode of the book club show—
your episode—happens to fall during sweeps month, when ratings are mea-
sured so as to figure how much to charge for advertising time, and since the
viewership for the monthly show featuring the book and the author always
plummets, the producers have decided to spend the first half of the hour
with bloopers from past shows. "Forgettable moments," these fragments
have been called by the promotional ads leading up to the air date.

This was what you were warned of, two weeks ago when you were
through with the taping. Officials from the show told you all this, and you'd
nodded, smiling, understanding. What else was there for you to do? De-
mand equal time with everyone else?

No. You'd nodded, smiled, understood.

Now the Force introduces video clip after video clip of, truly, forgettable moments from past episodes: two people argue over whether the toilet
paper is more efficiently utilized if rolled over the top or out from beneath;
a woman tells a Viagra joke; the Force marches down the street outside her
studio in protest of uncomfortable panty hose.

Your guests look at you.

"I had nothing to do with this," you say, too loud. "It'll be on the last
half of the show," you say, too loud again.

They are quiet for a while, then return to ladling dip onto plates, loading up wings and poppers, pouring soda, until, finally, you are introduced,
and the book, and there you are for two minutes talking about your grandmother, and your aunt with Down Syndrome, your voice clear and calm,
and you are amazed at how clear and calm you are there on the television, when you had wanted nothing more than to jump from the sofa you
were seated on in the studio and do jumping jacks to work off the fear and

trembling inside you. Now comes a series of family photos, a montage of images with your voice over it all, calm and smooth, the images on the screen of pictures your family has had for years.

Pictures of your grandmother, and of your aunt.

The people you wrote about whose lives are now here for the world to see, and you realize in this moment that you had nothing to do with this. That these photos—of your grandmother, your aunt, and your grandfather and aunts and uncles and your father too, all these family photos that have existed for years—simply bear testament to the fact they were lives lived out of your hands, and all you had to do was to write them down, getting credit for all those lives led.

You think about that bad day in January. About how this all began, and how all this credit has come to you.

Yet you are still a little steamed about losing the first half of the show, when every other author you've seen featured on the show has gotten most of the program. You are a little steamed, too, about not having some place to sit here in your living room, and about those kids banging on the keyboard. You are a little steamed.

Then the discussion with you and the four women and the Force begins, and you see, along with everyone in your house, and everyone in the country, the world, a discussion that had lasted three hours squelched down to eight minutes, and six or so of those given to a woman who gave up her Down Syndrome child at birth because of the "life sentence" she saw being handed her. You see in your living room choked with your friends this woman crying over her life, her decision, and see her somehow thank you for your book and the meaning it has given her life.

You knew this is what would be included on the air. You'd known it the moment her voice wavered and cracked that afternoon two weeks ago, there in the studio. You knew it then, and now here it is: this woman, crying over giving up her baby, and thanking you for it.

And you see yourself nod on the air, looking thoughtful.

She makes great TV, you think. This woman who missed the point of your book entirely.

‹ఞ›

2

You are answering the phones for a while, because of the terrible thing that has happened this bright, cold January day.

"We'll send you a brochure," you say to someone on the other end of the line, no one you know, and as she tells you her address, you do not write it down, only sit with your back to the desk, looking out the window onto the late afternoon world outside: snow, sky.

A little after lunch, this day turned very bad, a turn that has led to you here, in the office of the program in which you teach a thousand miles from home, to answer the phone for the administrative director.

She is in the other room, too much in shards to answer the phone, to field the bonehead questions that still come to a program such as this one no matter what bad things happen and when. People still call to ask about the program, about costs and applications, about credits and teachers. About all things.

Earlier today, before you began answering the phone, before lunch, your agent called here, where you are teaching others to write because it seems you know something about writing, to tell you the novel you have just finished writing is awful.

You are here for two weeks, in workshops and seminars, lectures and readings, the students, adults who know what is at stake. Though they have lives away from here, just as you have your own, you and they converge on this New England campus from all over the country, the world, twice a year to study the word and all it can mean. They come here to study writing, because they want to write, and some of them become friends to you and to the other writers teaching here, because it is this love of the word that unites you all.

Some of them become your friends.

Your agent said to you this morning, "What happened to this?" She said, "Where was your heart?"

Her call, you'd recognized with her words and tone, had not surprised you. You knew it was coming. You knew the book was dead and gone to hell in a handbasket, had known it for the last month as you'd tried to get to the end of the thing. You knew it had gone to hell in a handbasket even before you missed the deadline last week.

You knew.

The novel: a sequel to the last one you published, early last year. That one had done well, better than any of the others you've published this far. A novel you'd had a tough time trying to get published, seeing as how your books have never done that well. You're a literary author, and publishers know that means you don't sell many books. You're not a bestseller, they know. You write well enough, but you're just not a bestseller, a fact you reconciled yourself to many years ago.

But the first hardcover run of this latest book—a run in the low five figures—sold out in a few months, the publisher electing not to reprint. They'd sold as many as they'd believed they could sell, had also sold it to paperback with another publisher.

With selling out the print run, everything was great. So great they asked ten months ago if you would write a sequel to it, and you agreed, though it wasn't anything you'd thought much about. Not until you saw how well the book was selling.

Now, here you were, ten months later, teaching people to write on a day cursed with the sad and empty curse of a startlingly blue winter sky. A day in which you have been informed of what you have known all along: this one didn't work.

You know nothing about writing.

But this is not the bad thing. It had seemed bad enough to you, walking across campus to lunch after the phone call, three hours long, from your agent; a phone call in which you both reconnoitered the train wreck before you, pieced out what was salvageable, shrugged over what was lost.

The day seemed bad enough then.

And then.

Then, after lunch, one of the students was found in his room, dead. Not one of the students, but one of your students.

Not one of your students, but a friend.

Some of them become your friends.

You were to have had dinner in town with him tonight, to talk about the novel he is writing, the novel you had been working on with him all last semester, when he was a student of yours and during which time he became a friend. A big, ambitious, strange and haunting novel.

A novel that will go unfinished now.

He was found in his dorm room, sitting at his desk, having gone to his room the night before, students have said, complaining of a headache.

He was found sitting at his desk, reading a copy of one of your books. A novel. A lesser known one, one it seemed no one really cared for.

Your friend was reading it.

He was found at one thirty on this blue and cursed January afternoon. Now it is four o'clock, between that time and this a somber and hushed chaos breaking out all over campus. Everyone here knows everyone here. No one has ever died here before. He was too young. He was your friend.

And now you are answering phones for the administrative director who is in the other room. You told her you wanted to answer the phone to give her time away from the bonehead questions, but you know you offered as a means to keep yourself from falling into shards of your own. You offered, so that you would have something to do, and not have to think of this very bad day, when the loss of your own book, you see, means nothing. A book means nothing.

You have lost a friend. A friend who is here, a thousand miles from home, too. A friend not much older than you, his death a complete and utter surprise. He lives with his mother, you know, where he takes care of her, an invalid, and where he is writing a big, ambitious, strange and haunting novel.

The phone rings. You are looking out the window at the afternoon sky growing dark, the blue gone to an ashen violet, and you turn to the phone, watch it a moment as though its ringing might change how it appears, like in cartoons when the phone jumps from its place and shivers.

It rings, and nothing happens, rings again, and you pick up the receiver, hold it to your ear knowing another bonehead question is on its way.

"May I speak to _____ _____?" a man says, all business, a solid voice that carries authority with it, and you think perhaps this is an official from the college, calling on business. Not a bonehead.

"Hold on," you say, and place the phone down, go to the room next door, where she is sitting, gathering herself.

"Can you take a call?" you ask, and try to smile. "It's for you," you say, and she nods, sniffs, tries at a smile herself. She stands, and you follow her back into her office, her domain, you only a brief tenant this afternoon of a very bad day.

She picks up the phone, says, "Hello?" and her eyes go immediately to you. "You were just talking to him," she says, and hands you the phone, trying to smile.

You take the receiver, bring it to your ear, say, "Yes?"

"I'm calling from Chicago," the businessman's voice says to you, "and my boss is working on a project she needs to talk to you about. I need to break her from a meeting. Can you hold?"

A meeting, you think. My boss. What is this about?

You say, "Sure," and now music comes on the line, and you glance up at the director, who is looking at you, wondering too, you can see, what this might be about. You don't live here. You're a thousand miles from home. Who knows you are here, and why?

You shrug at her in answer to her eyes, and then the music stops with a phone connection click, and a voice you think you may recognize says your name, then her own, then shouts, "We're going to have so much fun!"

Who is this? Is this who you think it is? Is this who she says she is? Is this her?

"Is this a joke?" you shout. "Is this for real?" and your eyes quick jump to the director, who sits in a chair across from you, watching you in wonder.

This makes the woman calling—her—laugh, and she assures you this is no joke, this is for real, and that she has chosen a book you have written as her book of the month next month.

It's a book four books ago, a book out of print. A book about your grandmother, her Down Syndrome daughter, your family.

This isn't happening. It hasn't happened. It will not happen.

But it has happened: you have been chosen. Your book has been anointed.

"This is secret," she says. "You can't tell anyone. We'll announce it in twelve days. But you can't tell anyone."

"Can I tell my wife?" you manage to get out, and she laughs, says you can, but that's all, and she talks a little more, and you talk, and you cannot believe that you are talking to her, you here a thousand miles from home and with a secret larger than any you have ever had lain upon you. Even bigger.

Yet all you can think to say to her is, A friend of mine died today. A friend of mine died. Can I tell you a friend of mine died?

But you do not say it. You merely talk with her, her, about things you won't be able to recall five minutes from now.

And then the phone call is over, and you hang up, look at the administrative director.

She knows who it was, you can tell. She knows, but asks, "Was it her?"

"It's a secret," you say, your words hushed for fear someone else in the office might hear. "You can't tell anyone," you say, and you are standing, and you hug her because she is the closest person to you and you have this secret inside you, and because she is the only other person on the planet to know.

You will call your wife next. You will call her and tell her of this moment, of this delivery. Of this news beyond any news you have ever gotten.

You let go the director, and see she is crying, and you are crying now, too. You are crying, and you are smiling, and you look back to the window, see the ashen violet gone to a purple so deep and so true that you know none of this is happening, none of it. This is what you finally understand is surreal, a word you have heard and used a thousand times. But now it has meaning.

A friend has died. The Force has called. The sky has gone from a cold and indifferent blue to this regal purple. A secret has been bestowed. A novel has been lost. Another gone unfinished.

This is surreal.

You go to the window, lean against the frame, your face close enough to the glass to make out the intricate filaments of ice crystals there.

You want to feel the cold on your cheek, want evidence this is real, all of this day is real. You want evidence.

You listen again to her voice on the phone, the words exchanged. You feel this cold.

A friend has died, and you did not record his passing with the Force.

And now you cry openly, watching the sky out there in its regal color, regal not for anything you have done. Only assigned that value by your eyes on this particular January day. That color has nothing to do with you, exists as it does as a kind of gift whether you are here to see it or not.

What does a book matter?

Still you cry, and do not know if it is out of sorrow or joy, and decide in the next moment it is out of both.

⌀

1

Your newest book is pretty much going to hell. In a handbasket.

Late afternoon, December, and you and your wife are in lawn chairs at the soccer field, watching your younger son play in one of the last games before Christmas.

Christmas. Your deadline for the next novel. The advance you were given, a sum the same as you were paid for your last book, even though it sold out its print run and sold to paperback as well, was spent months ago. Ancient history. Now here's Christmas coming hard at you, the novel going to hell.

Your son, a wing, is out on the field, your wife sitting beside you on your left, your older son a few feet farther to your left and in a lawn chair too, and talking to a schoolmate sitting on the grass beside him. Long shadows fall from across the field toward you, cast by the forest there. Other parents, schoolmates, brothers and sisters are spread across your side of the field, those shadows approaching you all. Maybe thirty or forty people altogether. It's a small school, new and with no field on campus, this one a municipal field at a city park. Lawn chairs are the best anyone can do.

And of course here with you, too, is your book pretty much going to hell, and this fact, its lack of momentum in your head and heart coupled with that looming deadline, might as well be a dead body propped in yet another lawn chair sitting next to you for all its palpable presence in your life. The world knows, it seems to you, that you are flailing.

You are cranky. That's what you would like to think it is. But it is more than that, and you know it, and your wife knows it, and your children do, too. You are angry, resentful. You are in the last fifty pages, but the book is leaving you, not like sand through your fingers, but like ground glass swallowed down.

You believed you had something, going into its writing nine months ago. You believed you were headed somewhere.

You thought you knew something: that you could write this book.

So, when you see your son lag behind on a run downfield, you yell at him, "Get on the ball! Run! Get in the game!"

It's too loud, you know, with the first word out of your mouth, and you turn to your wife, say, "Why doesn't he get into the game?" as though to lend your outburst credence. As though to find in her some kind of agreement that it's your son slacking off, when you know too well it's about a book you are writing going down like ground glass.

She looks at you out the corner of her eye, says nothing.

Your older son gets up from his lawn chair and moves even farther away with his friend, and you look at him, too. He's got on sunglasses, a ball cap on backwards. He's embarrassed by you, you know.

You would have been, too, were you him.

But the book is dying. It is dying.

You yell, even louder, "Let's GO! Get in the GAME!" and feel your hands in fists on the arms of the lawn chair.

This time your younger son looks over his shoulder, though far downfield, and his eyes meet yours. Then, quickly, they dart away, to others on the sidelines, then to the ground, his back fully to you now, him running and running.

"He's always just hanging back like that," you say to your wife, quieter but, you only now realize, with your teeth clenched. "It's like he's always just watching what's going on." You know your words as you speak them are one more attempt to give your anger, your resentment a clear conscience: you're yelling because of your kid. Not because of you.

And now your wife stands, picks up her lawn chair, moves away, settles her chair a good fifty feet from you.

This is no signal to you of the embarrassment you are. It is nothing cryptic you are meant to decipher. It is her truth and yours both, big and dumb: you are a fool.

And it is because of a book. A stupid book. There are more important things, she is shouting to you in settling her lawn chair that far from you. There are more important things than a book.

You are here in your chair, alone with yourself. And the corpse of your book propped beside you.

You look off to the right, for no good reason but that it's away from those you have embarrassed; those who know you for the fool you are.

And see there near the sideline, almost to the corner of the field, a blond kid, down on one knee on the sideline, his back to you. He's maybe ten yards away, the sun falling across the field to give his blond hair an extra shimmer to it, turning it almost white.

He's talking to himself, you hear, his voice quiet but there, just there. He's got on a black T-shirt, cargo shorts, skateboard shoes, and though his back is to you, you can see he has in one hand a plastic yellow baseball bat, in the other a plastic Day-glo orange squirt gun.

He's holding them oddly, you can see, the bat by the thick end, where the ball makes contact, the handle up and perpendicular to the ground, like a flagstaff with no flag; the squirt gun he holds delicately, thumb and first finger at the bottom of the grip, as though it might be too hot.

He's still talking, and you can see the gun and bat moving a little, first the gun, his hand shaking it in sync, you hear, with his words, then the bat, the movement small, like the sound of his voice coming to you across the grass, and over the shouts of players at the far end of the field. Then the gun shakes again, and you see too by the movement of his head that he looks at the gun when he moves it and talks, and looks as well at the bat when he moves it and talks.

What is he doing?

Then he turns, rolls toward you from the knee he is on to sitting flat on the ground. He's facing you now, still holding the bat and gun in this odd way, and you see, now, now, he is a Down Syndrome boy: almond eyes, thick neck, his mouth open.

He speaks again, looks at the bat, moving it with his words, and you only now realize he is speaking for the bat, that the bat itself is talking, this boy supplying the words, and then the gun answers the bat.

They are talking one to the other: a yellow bat, a Day-glo squirt gun.

The boy is about your younger son's age, you see, and see too the shimmer of late afternoon sunlight in his hair the same as a few moments before, when his back was to you, and you hadn't known. You hadn't known.

You look at him. Still they talk one to the other, the words nothing you can make out, but there is something beautiful and profound in what you see. Something right and simple and true, and just past your understanding.

It's a kind of peace you see, and can't understand, this moment.

I wrote a book about that, you think. I wrote a book about a Down Syndrome person, my aunt, and her mother. My grandmother, you think.

That was a good book, you think. That one was a gift, given to you without your even asking.

A gift, you think, and you wonder who this boy is with, who his own family is, who he is a gift to, and just as you wonder this you hear a rise in the crowd.

Parents and children in lawn chairs are growing louder now, clapping, hollering, though nothing as bombastic as what you knew you let out a few minutes before, and you turn to the sound, see your son's team moving and moving before the goal down there, the ball popped to the left and then right, and now you hear from the boy the word, "Go," then louder, "Go! GO!" and you look at him, see him turned to that end of the field now too, see the bat and gun held still, this boy back up on one knee and in profile to you. "GO JOHNNY!" he yells, and you know he has a brother out there.

The gun and bat talk to one another again, while the shadows from the far side of the field grow closer to you all, to everyone, and now you know you knew nothing in writing that book. It was a gift, this story of a mother and daughter, but has it made you a better father to your son? Has it made you a better husband to your wife?

The answer, of course, is no, because here you are, chewing out the world around you because a book is going down like ground glass swallowed.

This is when the boy happens to glance up from the dialogue he creates and lives at once, to see you looking at him. Your eyes meet for a moment, the talking toys now still, and you say, "Hi." You say it just to be nice to him. You say it because your eyes have met, and he has seen you watching him.

But you say it to try and save yourself.

He looks at you, looks at you, and even before he goes back to the dialogue at hand, his friends these toys, you know he won't say a thing.

You are a stranger.

You look beside you. There is no corpse of a book here, not anywhere around. Your wife is gone too, her to your left and away from you, your older son even farther away. And there is your younger son, out on the field and running away from you as best he can. Your son, a teammate to this boy's brother.

There is, you know, only you here with you, and though you wish it were possible, pray it might be possible, there is no way for you to stand and lift your lawn chair and walk fifty feet away from you.

Which is what you want to do. To be away from you, here.

Because you have been blessed.

You have been blessed.

You have been blessed.

❧

0

You have everything to learn.

This will be what keeps you. What points you toward humility: knowing how very little you know, how very far you have to go. As far now, in

the second person and once it's all over, as on an afternoon soccer field,
shadows growing long.

I know nothing. I know I know nothing.

I have been blessed.

for Jim Ferry

Sources (In Order Cited)

Chapter 1: What's a Heaven For?

Arelius, Marcus, and Maxwell Staniforth. *Meditations*. New York: Penguin, 1985.

Wu, Duncan. *Victorian Poetry*. Oxford: Blackwell, 2002.

Trudeau, G. B. *Doonesbury's Greatest Hits*. New York: Holt, Rinehart and Winston, 1978.

Tuleja, Elizabeth A. *Intercultural Communication for Business*. Mason, OH: South-Western Cengage Learning, 2008.

Chapter 2: What I Learned in Lent

LePore, Jill. "The Divider." *New Yorker*, March 17, 2008.

Lorenz, Lee. Cartoon. *New Yorker*, June 25, 2007.

Fields, Leslie Leyland. "The Case for Kids." *Christianity Today*, August 2006.

Bonds, Barry. Cable News Network, November 16, 2008.

Http://www.cybernation.com/quotations.

Nouwen, Henri. *The Genesee Diary*. New York: Doubleday/Image, 1981.

Oxford English Dictionary. Oxford: Oxford University Press.

Buechner, Frederick. *Wishful Thinking: A Theological ABC*. San Francisco: HarperOne, 1993.

Shaw, Luci. *Harvesting Fog*. Montrose, CO: Pinyon, 2010.

Economist. "Dandy Dames." Review of *Dangerous Ambition: Rebecca West and Dorothy Thompson; New Women in Search of Love and Power*, by Susan Hertog. *Economist*, November 8, 2011.

The New Shorter Oxford English Dictionary. New York: Oxford University Press, 1993.

Berry, Wendell. *Sex, Economy and Freedom*. New York: Pantheon, 1994.

Hall, Donald. From a lecture given at the Calvin Festival of Faith and Writing, Grand Rapids, Michigan, 2000.

Hall, Donald. *Unpacking the Boxes*. New York: Houghton Mifflin, 2008.

Disraeli, Benjamin. See http://www.lifequoteslib.com/authors/benjamin_disraeli_7.html.

Mariani, Paul. *Gerard Manley Hopkins: A Life*. New York: Penguin/Viking, 2008.

Volf, Miroslav. *Exclusion and Embrace*. Nashville: Abingdon, 1996.

Lewis, C. S. *Mere Christianity*. New York: Collier/Macmillan, 1978.

Frayn, Michael. *Copenhagen*. New York: Anchor/Random House, 1998.

Chapter 3: The Lure of Fame: The Yearning, the Drive, the Question Mark

Milton, John. "Lycidas." In *The Complete Poetical Works of John Milton*. Edited by Harry Francis Fletcher. New York: Houghton Mifflin Harcourt, 1941.

Shakespeare, William. *The Tragedy of Julius Caesar.* Act 4, scene 2. Edited by William Montgomery. New York: Penguin, 1960.

Comden, Betty, and Adolph Green. "Make Someone Happy." Stratford Music Corporation. Stratford Music Limited, 1960.

Plato. "Apology 38A." In *Plato in Twelve Volumes.* Vol. 1. Translated by Harold North Fowler. Cambridge: Harvard University Press, 1966.

Wilde, Oscar. http://thinkexist.com/quotation/i_regard_the_theatre_as_the_greatest_of_all_art/217546.html.

Chapter 4: Ye Shall Be as Gods

Housman, A. E. "To an Athlete Dying Young." In *A Shropshire Lad.* New York: Avon, 1950.

Shakespeare, William. *The History of Troilus and Cressida.* Act 3, scene 3. In *The Riverside Shakespeare,* edited by G. Blakemore Evans. Boston: Houghton Mifflin, 1974.

Dante. *La Divina Commedia di Dante Alighieri.* Vol. 1. *Inferno.* Florence: Sansoni, 1945.

Milton, John. *Paradise Lost.* Book 1. New York: Collier, 1962.

Shakespeare, William. *The Famous History of the Life of Henry the Eighth.* Act 2, scene 2. *The Riverside Shakespeare.* Boston: Houghton Mifflin, 1974.

Tocqueville, Alexis de. *Democracy in America.* Vols. 1 & 2. Everyman's Library. New York: Borzoi/Knopf, 1994.

Machiavelli, Niccolo. *The Prince.* Introduction by Harvey C. Mansfield Jr. Chicago: University of Chicago Press, 1985.

Chapter 5: Ambition: Lilies That Fester

Shakespeare, William. "Sonnet 94." http://www.shakespeare-online.com/sonnets/94.html.

Hopkins, Gerard Manley. *The Poems of Gerard Manley Hopkins.* 4th ed. Edited by W. H. Gardner and N. H. Mackenzie. London: Oxford University Press, 1967.

Von Hugel, Friedrich. *Letters to a Niece.* London: Dent, 1958. Quoted at http://thequoteables.blogspot.com/2008/03/no-dittos.html.

Berry, Wendell. *The Gift of Good Land.* San Francisco: North Point, 1981.

Berry, Wendell. *Home Economics.* San Francisco: North Point, 1987.

Clarke, James Freeman. *Self-Culture.* Repr. ed. Whitefish, MT: Kessinger, 2006.

Chargaff, Earwin. *Heraclitean Fire.* New York: Rockefeller University Press, 1978.

Dubie, Norman. "The Czar's Last Christmas Letter: A Barn in the Urals." In *The Mercy Seat: Collected & New Poems 1967–2001.* Port Townsend, WA: Copper Canyon, 2004.

Forsythe, Peter. *The Cure of Souls.* Edited by Harry Escott. Grand Rapids, MI: Eerdmans, 1971.

Chapter 7: Dreams Are Dangerous; They Uncover Your Bones

Shackleton Exhibit at the National Geographic Museum in Washington, DC.

NBC News. August 12, 2012.

Chapter 8: Why Run When You Can Fly?

Http://en.wikipedia.org/wiki/Grete_Waitz.

Http://en.wikipedia.org/wiki/List_of_Evel_Knievel_career_jumps.

Http://www.guinnessworldrecords.com/records-11000/most-broken-bones-in-a-lifetime.

Http://www.nytimes.com/2007/12/01/us/01knievel.html?pagewanted=all.

Bradley, Bill. http://thinkexist.com/quotation/ambition_is_the_path_to_success-persistence_is/200886.html.

Peary, Robert. *Northward Over the Great Ice*. Vol. 1. New York: Stokes, 1898.

Loomis, Chauncy. *Weird and Tragic Shores*. New York: Modern Library, 2000.

Hall, Charles. *Arctic Researches and Life among the Esquimaux*. Washington, DC: Government Printing Office, 1879.

About the Authors

Scott Cairns

Scott Cairns, Professor of English at University of Missouri, co-directs writing workshops in Greece. His poems and essays have appeared in *Poetry, Image, Paris Review, The Atlantic Monthly, The New Republic*, etc., and both have been anthologized in *Best American Spiritual Writing*. His most recent books are *Slow Pilgrim: The Collected Poems, Short Trip to the Edge*, and *The End of Suffering*. He is a recipient of a Guggenheim Fellowship and the Denise Levertov Award.

‐

Diane Glancy

Diane Glancy is professor emeritus at Macalester College in St. Paul, Minnesota. She was the 2008–09 Richard Thomas Professor at Kenyon College in Gambier, Ohio, and a 2012–14 visiting professor at Azusa Pacific University near Los Angeles. Her latest poetry collections, *Stories of the Driven World* and *It Was Then*, were published by Mammoth Press in 2010 and 2012. Her latest collection of nonfiction, *The Dream of a Broken Field*, was published by the University of Nebraska Press in 2011. She is at work on a new collection of nonfiction, *An Act of Disobedience*, which is about maintaining faith in a secular world. Her 2014–15 books are *Fort Marion Prisoners and the Trauma of Native Education*—nonfiction, *Report to the Department of the Interior*—poetry, and three novels—*Uprising of Goats, One of Us*, and *Ironic Witness*.

The Autry National Center in Los Angeles produced her fourth play, *The Bird House*, during their 2013 season. The play centers on fracking, a process of drilling for natural gas that injects carcinogens into the ground to break up shale beds. Glancy took the idea of fracking into the lives of the characters. Reverend Hawk is fracked by the downsizing of his congregation in Ropesville, Texas, because they had to move to other areas for work. Hawk's sister, Clovis, is fracked by a stroke. He also has a half-sister, Majel, whose Native American heritage is fracked by assimilation. The land around Hawk is fracked by the process of fracking until well water is polluted and he has to buy bottled water. He also comes to realize that Christ suffered fracking on the cross when he took the sins of humanity upon himself.

Glancy is the recipient of two National Endowment for the Arts Fellowships, a Minnesota Book Award, an Oklahoma Book Award, and an American Book Award from the Before Columbus Foundation. She received a 2012 Distinguished Alumni Award from the University of Missouri.

She lived near the foothills in Monrovia, California, where a bear sometimes rattled the trash cans until May 2014 when she returned to her permanent home in Shawnee Mission, Kansas. Her websites are www.dianeglancy.com and www.dianeglancy.org.

⊷

Emilie Griffin

Emilie is a writer and speaker and the author of a number of books on the spiritual life. Most recent are *Souls in Full Sail* (Christianity Today award 2011) and *Green Leaves for Later Years: The Spiritual Path of Wisdom* (October 2012).

She is a poet and playwright who has written a number of books, especially focusing on prayer and the power of reflection. Two new collections of her poems and plays are planned for 2014 and 2016. She writes for *America*, is a founding member of The Chrysostom Society, and is active with the Renovaré movement for spiritual renewal. Working with the Renovaré Institute has given her the chance to teach Augustine, Aquinas, and Aristotle; explore her love of the poetry of Shakespeare, Herbert, Donne, and Hopkins; and to clown around on stage with the likes of Richard Foster and Dallas Willard.

Emilie is married to author, editor, and humorist William Griffin, and together they are the parents of three grown children and grandparents of four. She and William are active in the Writers Guild of Central Louisiana and Spectral Sisters Productions, a theater group that develops and produces original plays.

A New Orleans native, Emilie worked in New York City for twenty years. She holds a BA in English and classics from Newcomb College, was elected to Phi Beta Kappa, and has done graduate work in theology at Loyola New Orleans and Notre Dame Seminary, and Spanish literature at National University of Mexico. She edited The Chrysostom Society book on writing, *A Syllable of Water*, and has contributed to several volumes of Christian religious history.

⇢

Bret Lott

Bret Lott read his brains out when he was a kid, but never gave being a writer a thought. What he really wanted to be was a forest ranger, riding a horse through a national park and telling people to be careful with campfires. But after a bad semester in the forestry program at Northern Arizona University, and then another bad semester in a physics course at California State Long Beach, he dropped out of school, became an RC Cola salesman, and believed he'd sell soda pop the rest of his days. It only took a year for him to realize that wasn't what he wanted to do, so he took a class at a community college to get prepped for going back to the university. The only night he had free was Tuesday, and the only course open that night was Creative Writing. Eight years later his first novel—*The Man Who Owned Vermont*, about the life and times of an RC Cola salesman—was published. On occasion he still dreams of riding a horse through the woods, but it seems the whole writing thing has worked out pretty well.

⇢

Erin McGraw

A native of southern California, Erin McGraw attended college in Davis, California, moved to the Midwest in the 1980s, and now considers herself a born-again Midwesterner. In this role she spends a good deal of time explaining to friends and family how the flyover states are hipper than anyone thinks, a true assertion backed up by surprisingly good clubs, even better restaurants, and affordable parking all over town.

She is the author of six books of fiction, including a new novel, *Better Food for a Better World* (Slant Books, 2013), and has received fellowships from Stanford University and the Corporation of Yaddo as well as grants from the Ohio Arts Council. With her husband, the poet Andrew Hudgins, and two ill-mannered dogs, she divides her time between Columbus, Ohio, where she teaches fiction writing at Ohio State University, and Sewanee, Tennessee, where she grumbles about the deer eating her garden.

Her essays and stories have appeared in the *Atlantic Monthly*, the *Southern Review*, STORY, *Good Housekeeping*, *Allure*, the *Kenyon Review*, the *Gettysburg Review*, and many other journals and magazines. When she is not writing, she tends to be reading about food, but not cooking it; watching sports on TV, but not playing them; listening to music, but not performing it. She has ambitions, however, to get cracking on all of these very soon.

⤝

Gina Ochsner

Having just finished a novel set in Eastern Latvia that involves eels, the fine art of mushroom hunting, a recurring problem with bodies in cemeteries, and little boys with enormous furry ears, I'm turning my imagination to places farther east. Specifically, I'm interested in Moldova. I said this to a friend who lives in Central Russia. The weather at the time happened to be −40°C. "Why in the world would you want to write about Moldova?" she asked. "Because in Moldova it's not −40°," I said. But the real reason is that like so many countries, Moldova is a complicated blend of people, ethnicities, languages, and cultures. And like every country, Moldova has a strange and haunted history that begs repeating, though nobody tells the story exactly the same way twice. This is what fascinated me most: the inherent contradiction between individual and collective memory.

Eugene H. Peterson

Pastor John of Patmos provided the biblical DNA that gave me an integrated vocation of pastor/writer. The apocalyptic angel who delivered the vision to John as he worshiped on that memorable Lord's Day said, "Write in a book what you see . . ." *Write what you see.* Writer and pastor were two sides of a single identity for John. It was not as if he added writer onto his vocation as pastor or pastor onto his vocation as writer. Pastor was not his "day job" and writer, the work for which he is best known today his "real job." Nor was pastor, the work for which he was best known in his own seven churches, and writer a mere moonlighting diversion. Writer and pastor were the same thing for John. Right foot, left foot: pastor, writer. Not writer competing for time from pastor. Not pastor struggling to integrate writer into an already crowded schedule. Pastor/Writer, a single coherent identity for John, and for me, Eugene.

Under the influence of John and his *Revelation* I began to understand and practice a way of writing that was at some deeper level a conversation with Scripture. At the same time it was a conversation with my congregation. But it was conversation; not explaining, not directing. I was exploring the country, this land of the living. And I was taking my time. It was a way of writing that involved a good deal of listening, looking around, getting acquainted with the neighborhood. Not writing what I knew but writing into what I didn't know, edging into mystery.

Novelist Kurt Vonnegut described this writing as walking through a dense forest in the dead of night with a pencil flashlight between your teeth, about two feet of darkness before you as you worked your way from word to word. True for me, too.

❧

Luci Shaw

Luci was born in 1928 to missionary parents, whose peregrinations took her around the planet from her earliest years and enrolled her in a series of schools with conflicting educational systems. This was said to have enriched her life but left her in a cloud of unknowing with regard to algebra. During her growing up she did a lot of reading and kept a journal. In the 1950s, at Wheaton College, her penchant for writing was tamed and set free. She graduated with high honors and got married five days later. Five children arrived soon thereafter, and her evenings were occupied with freelance editing. With her husband Harold she soon started a publishing house, and as senior editor she tangled with J. I. Packer, Madeleine L'Engle, Thomas Howard, and dozens of others.

Harold and Luci became Episcopalians just before his death, a community that has anchored her ever since. In 1987 she was invited to be writer in residence at Regent College, where she taught poetry and reflective journal-keeping to gifted graduate students. Her own peregrinations have taken her to arts conferences in a variety of cities and countries. She has published about thirty-three books of poetry and essays (but who's counting?), as well as editing *festschrifts* and other exotica. Three new books are in the pipeline.

Along with good friends like Madeleine L'Engle, Richard Foster, Emilie Griffin, and Philip Yancey, she founded something called The Chrysostom (Golden Mouth) Society in 1986. This was a fine thing that over time grew to be even finer. Together these writers have shared the triumphs as well as the urgencies and agonies of their writing lives and commiserated when their books were overlooked or remaindered. They also indulge in clerihews and bad limericks at each others' expense. Meeting every year, their real job is to encourage younger writers, write books that engage with current culture, and keep tabs on each other by publishing collaborative volumes, endorsing each others' writings, and showing up to heckle at each others' readings.

Luci was grateful to receive the Denise Levertov Award from *Image* and Seattle Pacific University in 2013. And for reasons that seem good to her alma mater, her letters and papers are being collected at Wheaton College.

She is now married to John Hoyte, and between them they have a tribe of seven children, ten grandchildren, and two really great-grandchildren.

For further excitements check Luci's web site:

http://www.lucishaw.com.

ᘒ

Dain Trafton

Dain Trafton considers himself lucky to have grown up in the rough and tumble world he describes in his contribution to this volume. From the unglamorous mill town in central Maine where he had his beginnings, he had the good fortune, guided by his parents, to go on to an excellent boarding school (very rough and tumble), where he played violent sports and learned why "The Windhover" is a finer poem than "Gunga Din" and *Crime and Punishment* is a greater novel than *The Last of the Mohicans*, although he has never lost his love of Rudyard Kipling or James Fenimore Cooper. A story he wrote about a boy growing up in the 1940s who loses Eden all over again won a school prize.

At college, where running his motorcycle into a truck put an end to his (not very promising) career in violent sports, he majored in English, wrote some bad poetry and fiction, and got married. In graduate school (still studying English) he found himself drawn especially to Shakespeare and Milton and their Italian, French, Spanish, and classical antecedents. A thesis on Shakespeare's history plays led to an academic career at various institutions in the United States and abroad, which—though not all bliss (especially a rough and tumble stint as an academic dean)—provided on the whole a very satisfying blend of reading, teaching, and writing.

Dain has published scholarly and critical writings on works in various languages, translations (from Italian into English), fiction, poetry, and essays aimed at a general audience. Currently retired (and still married to his college sweetheart), he lives in the western mountains of Maine, where he works mainly on his fiction and poetry. A motive that informs much of his work as a teacher and writer is the desire to conserve beautiful and profound old things—including things from the Christian tradition—that are in danger of being forgotten or devalued. Readers of his contribution to this volume may wonder, Does Dain Trafton long to be "as a god"? Of course he does, but he prays to be forgiven.

◆

Jeanne Murray Walker

Jeanne Murray Walker was born in a village of seven hundred in Northern Minnesota, where her father's family opened the town's general store after arriving from Sweden. Growing up in the Midwest after her father died, Jeanne became adept at avoiding canning and sewing and cleaning in order to read and practice the violin. These bad habits led eventually to graduate school and to a life of writing.

Jeanne has taught English at the University of Delaware since 1975 and also serves as a mentor in the Seattle Pacific University Master of Fine Arts Program. Her plays have been produced around this country and in London, and her poetry has been featured on busses and trains. An Atlantic Monthly Fellow at Bread Loaf School of English, Jeanne has also been honored with a National Endowment for the Arts Fellowship, eight Pennsylvania Council on the Arts Fellowships, and a Pew Fellowship in the Arts. Her work has recently been reprinted in *The Open Door: 100 Poets, 100 Years of Poetry*, an anthology celebrating the centennial of *Poetry* magazine. Her memoir, *Geography of Memory: A Pilgrimage into Alzheimer's* was published in 2013 and in 2014 Word Farm Press brought out *Helping the Morning: New and Selected Poems*. Jeanne's website is www.JeanneMurrayWalker.com.

Jeanne is the mother of two children and three grandchildren. When she is not at home with her lawyer husband in Philadelphia, she lectures, teaches, and gives readings in places ranging from the Library of Congress and Oxford University, to Whidbey Island and Texas canyon country.

Acknowledgments

THE EDITORS, LUCI AND Jeanne, wish to acknowledge with enormous gratitude the detailed supervision and patient preparation of *Ambition* by Dain
Trafton and Lynda Graybeal that followed our earlier work of selecting and
editing. Without the steady dedication to perfection on the part of Dain
and Lynda, this book might never have seen the light of day. The editors
also wish to thank Robert Ayres, whose generosity has gone a long way
towards making this book possible, and Greg Wolfe, whose wise counsel
has made it better than it would otherwise have been.

What Is The Chrysostom Society?

In 1986 Richard Foster had a bright idea. He wanted to gather together
some writers to find out if they could accomplish more together than as
individuals. His intention, announced in his letter of invitation to new
members, was "to consider the feasibility of establishing a National Guild
of Professional Writers" whose literary efforts flowed out of the Christian
worldview.

Soon twelve writers met at Christ Haven, a retreat center near Colo-
rado Springs. From that time forward, the group has met annually. Members have come and gone, but numbers have stayed between twenty to
twenty-five.

The group has included Baptists, Christian Reformed, Church of
God, Anglicans, Episcopalians, Lutherans, Prebyterians, Quakers, Eastern Orthodox, and Roman Catholics. To meet the members, log on to
http:\\www.chrysostomsociety.org.

The authors who make up the group include poets, playwrights, novelists, critics, biographers, and spiritual writers. In its early days, the group
took the name "The Chrysostom Society," recalling John Chrysostom,
whose name means "golden-mouthed," who is among the greatest of the

Greek fathers of the Church. Born in about AD 347, he died in 407 and in 451, at the Council of Chalcedon, he was declared a Doctor of the Church.